ITALY PROFILED

ITALY
PROFILED

Essential facts on society, business and politics in Italy

Edited by Barry Turner

ST.MARTIN'S PRESS
NEW YORK

ITALY PROFILED

Copyright © 1999 by Barry Turner

St Martin's Press, Scholarly and Reference Division,
175 Fifth Avenue, New York, N.Y. 10010

First published in the United States of America in 1999

Printed in the United Kingdom

ISBN: 0–312–22724–8

Library of Congress Cataloging-in-Publication Data
Italy profiled / essential facts on society, business, and politics in
Italy / edited by Barry Turner.
    p. cm.
    Includes bibliographical references and index.
    ISBN 0–312–22724–8 (pbk.)
        1. Italy—Social life and customs. 2. National characteristics,
    Italian. 3. Political culture—Italy. 4. Italy—Intellectual life.
    5. Etiquette—Italy. I. Turner, Barry.

    DG441.19 1999
    945—dc21   99–050167

Contents

Colour maps fall between pages 112 and 113

ITALY

Repubblica Italiana

Capital: Rome

Area: 301,308 sq. km

Population estimate, 2000: 57·46m.

Head of State: Carlo Azeglio Ciampi

Head of Government: Massimo D'Alema

TERRITORY AND POPULATION

Italy is bounded in the north by Switzerland and Austria, east by
Slovenia and the Adriatic Sea, south-east by the Ionian Sea, south by
the Mediterranean Sea, south-west by the Tyrrhenian Sea and
Ligurian Sea and west by France. The area is 301,308 sq. km.
Populations at successive censuses were as follows:

10 Feb. 1901	33,370,138	4 Nov. 1951	47,158,738
10 June 1911	35,694,582	15 Oct. 1961	49,903,878
1 Dec. 1921	37,403,956	24 Oct. 1971	53,744,737
21 April 1931	40,582,043	25 Oct. 1981	56,335,678
21 April 1936	42,302,680	20 Oct. 1991	56,764,854

Population estimate, 1 Jan. 1998: 57,563,354 (29,612,762 females).
Density: 191 per sq. km.

The projected population for 2000 is 57·46m.

In 1995 an estimated 66·6% of the population lived in urban areas,
down slightly from 66·7% in 1990. Italy and Austria are the only
European countries to have had a decline in the proportion of the
population living in urban areas in the period 1990–95.

The following table gives area and population of the Autonomous Regions (census 1991 and estimate 1997):   .

Regions	Area in sq. km (1996)	Resident pop. census, 1991	Resident pop. 1997	Density per sq. km
Piedmont	25,399	4,302,565	4,291,441	169
Valle d'Aosta[1]	3,263	115,938	119,610	37
Lombardy	23,861	8,856,074	8,988,951	375
Trentino-Alto Adige[1]	13,607	90,360	924,281	68
Bolzano-Bozen	7,404	440,508	457,370	61
Trento	6,207	449,852	466,911	75
Veneto	18,379	4,380,797	4,469,156	242
Friuli-Venezia Giulia[1]	7,844	1,197,666	1,184,654	151
Liguria	5,421	1,676,282	1,641,835	305
Emilia Romagna	22,124	3,909,512	3,947,102	178
Tuscany	22,997	3,529,946	3,527,303	153
Umbria	8,456	811,831	831,714	98
Marche	9,693	1,429,205	1,450,879	149
Lazio	17,208	5,140,371	5,242,709	303
Abruzzi	10,799	1,249,054	1,276,040	118
Molise	4,438	330,90	329,894	75
Campania	13,595	5,630,280	5,796,899	426
Puglia	19,363	4,031,885	4,090,068	211
Basilicata	9,992	610,528	610,330	61
Calabria	15,080	2,070,203	2,070,992	138
Sicily[1]	25,707	4,966,386	5,108,067	198
Sardinia[1]	24,090	1,648,248	1,661,429	69

[1] With special statute.

Communes of more than 100,000 inhabitants, with population resident at the census of 20 Oct. 1991 and on 31 Dec.1996:

	1991	1996		1991	1996
Rome	2,775,250	2,645,322	Foggia	156,268	156,301
Milan	1,369,231	1,303,925	Salerno	148,932	143,751
Naples	1,067,365	1,045,874	Perugia	144,732	151,118
Turin	962,507	919,612	Ferrara	138,015	135,326
Palermo	698,556	687,855	Ravenna	135,844	134,297
Genoa	678,771	653,529	Reggio nell'Emilia	132,030	137,337
Bologna	404,376	385,136	Rimini	127,960	129,596
Florence	403,294	380,058	Syracuse	125,941	127,224
Bari	342,309	335,410	Sassari	122,339	121,412
Catania	333,075	341,455	Pescara	122,236	117,957
Venice	309,422	296,422	Monza	120,651	119,197
Verona	255,824	254,520	Bergamo	114,936	117,193
Taranto	232,334	211,660	Forli	109,541	107,827
Messina	231,693	262,224	Terni	108,248	108,432
Trieste	213,100	221,551	Vicenza	107,454	108,281
Padua	215,137	212,542	Latina	106,203	111,679
Cagliari	204,237	174,175	Piacenza	102,268	99,665
Brescia	194,502	189,767	Trento	101,545	103,474
Reggio di Calabria	177,580	180,034	La Spezia	101,442	97,712
Modena	176,990	175,124	Torre del Greco	101,361	97,438
Parma	170,520	167,504	Ancona	101,285	99,453
Livorno	167,512	163,950	Novara	101,112	102,408
Prato	165,707	168,892	Lecce	100,884	99,763

The official language is Italian, spoken by 94·1% of the population in 1991. There are 0·3m. German-speakers in Bolzano and 30,000 French-speakers in Valle d'Aosta.

In addition to Sicily and Sardinia, there are a number of other Italian islands, the largest being Elba (363 sq. km), and the most distant Lampedusa, which is 205 km from Sicily but only 113 km from Tunisia.

REGIONS

North West

Regions: Piedmont, Lombardy, Liguria, Val d'Aosta
Main Cities: Turin, Genoa, Aosta, Milan

Val d'Aosta

One of the smallest regions in Italy, Aosta is a region of alpine peaks and picturesque landscapes. In the 11th century, the kingdom of Val d'Aosta was part of Savoy-Piedmont. Situated on the invasion route from France, the area suffered many cross border intrusions and, until the end of the 19th century, the people of this region were French speaking. Aosta is the regional capital and is the centre of an important tourist area attracting an average of 6·5m. visitors, mostly in the winter months for the ski season. Val d'Aosta owes its prosperity to the export of 75% of its annual production of hydroelectric power to meet the heavy industrial demands of neighbouring Piedmont. Italy has few indigenous sources of energy and an increase in investment in the hydroelectric industry in this region is planned over the next decade.

Piedmont

(For more details on Milan and Turin see pages 83 and 89 respectively)
The kingdom of Savoy-Piedmont was founded by Umberto Biancamano and, like Val d'Aosta, it has suffered greatly from invading forces over the centuries. However, in the early years of the 18th century, during the war of the Spanish Succession, the Piedmontese under Duke Vittorio Amadeo II attacked the French who were marching

south to Lombardy. He not only gained Sicily but also was elevated to the status of King by the Treaty of Utrecht in 1714. Turin is the capital city of the region and has the historic distinction of having been at the centre of the Italian struggle for unity in the 19th century. The city was the home of the first Italian Parliament in 1861 after the unification of Italy. Piedmont commercial enterprises include the Fiat based automobile industry of Turin, Olivetti computers at Ivrea and textiles in Biella, as well as wine, soft fruits and agricultural produce from Alessandria and Novara. The industries of Piedmont are so highly automated and technologically advanced that high output is achieved with a relatively small work force (1·8m. – less than 9% of the Italian total) but Turin is moving away from its traditional industrial base towards banking, finance, service industries and technology. The area encompassed by Turin, Ivrea and Novara has been designated Italy's 'Techno-City' and hosts new high-tech industries including robotics, aerospace, telecommunications, computers, bioengineering and the development of new materials. Among the major names present in the Techno-city are Aeritalia (Aerospace and aviation), SKF (ball and roller bearing), Microtechnica (aviation and space research), Prima Industry, Bisiach and Carm (robotics), BICC/CEAT (cabling) and Pirelli (tyres). The province of Cuneo is one of the largest market garden areas of north Italy with soil and climate conditions that are perfect for the production of vegetables and soft fruits and Albi and Asti produce high quality wines. Alessandria and Valenza also produce jewellery while Vercelli is famous for the cultivation of rice and maize. The region is on the threshold of the Alps, close to France and the Italian Riviera.

Lombardy

Lombardy has dominated northern Italy for centuries and continues to do so today. The region has always been one of the battlefields of Europe and during the Thirty Years War (1618–48) the region was crossed and re-crossed by French, Spanish and Austrian troops who were fighting over Valtellina. This resulted in a long period of economic decline that was not reversed until the 18th century. In 1796, the French returned, this time under Napoleon Bonaparte who was crowned King of Italy in Milan in 1805. After Napoleon was defeated, the kingdom of Lombardy was absorbed into the Austrian Empire until Piedmont was unified with the rest of Italy in 1861. Lombardy is the most heavily populated region in Italy, and large numbers of the workforce have come from the south attracted by the higher wages and abundance of work in the factories around Milan. The heavily industrialized areas surrounding Milan produce 40% of Italy's GNP. The regional capital is the true economic and financial heart of Italy and has been a major trading and manufacturing centre for centuries. The wide range of industries to be found in and around Milan include steel, heavy engineering, machine tools, transport and transport equipment, chemicals, oil refining, plastics, textiles, clothing and shoes, electronics and domestic appliances. The food industry is strong in the area. Milan is also the centre of Italian design and fashion.

Liguria

(For more details on Genoa see page 94)

Liguria is a coastal strip that runs to the French border on the Mediterranean seaboard with Genoa as its main city and one of the principal ports of Italy. The region saw repeated invasions by the French and the Austrians during the 17th and 18th centuries and the fortunes of the once powerful and prosperous maritime kingdom went into a period of decline. Genoa was at the heart of the Italian industrial revolution in the late 19th century and the region produced the first Italian motor car, the first military field tank and the first Italian aeroplane. Liguria's wealth traditionally stemmed from the production of steel, port handling and shipbuilding, but today these industries are under threat. ILVA – a branch of the state controlled IRI – is planning to close its last remaining steel producing factories after suffering heavy losses, and the region is trying to attract high-tech industries and inward investment to the area. A new port is being created to replace the obsolete old port of Genoa to handle container traffic, oil and petrochemicals and an increased amount of ferry traffic. Tourism, once one of the area's main sources of income, is also on the decline although the coastal strip has many attractive small towns and resorts that are still popular in the summer. On the positive side, Liguria has one of the highest qualities of life in Italy (according to a survey conducted recently) and the purchasing power of the local population is boosted by a large number of wealthy people from other regions who have retired to the area. Oil and petro-chemical industries are thriving as is the small industries sector (30% of businesses registered with the Genoa Chamber of Commerce are run by women) and the region is served by excellent road and railway links (Genoa is on the Munich-Verona line). The region's GDP is in line with the national average.

In 1992, Genoa celebrated one of its famous sons with the Columbus Festival. Substantial inward investment was attracted to the region, much of which was used for urban renewal.

North East
Regions: Trentino-Alto-Adige, Veneto, Friuli-Veneto-Giulia, Emilia-Romagna.
Main Towns: Bolzano, Trento, Udine, Trieste, Cortina, Verona, Venice, Parma, Ferrara, Bologna, Ravenna.

Trentino-Alto-Adige
This alpine area to the north of Verona is a semi-autonomous section of the Veneto region. Trentino-Alto-Adige was part of the Austrian Empire until 1918 and German is still spoken in the region. Linguistic issues are an ongoing problem here with ethnic Germans still resenting what they see as the 'Italianization' of their region under Mussolini,

with Italian place names replacing German ones. On the other hand, the Ladins (the Italian population) claim that their origins go back to the Romans and want their Italian language rights protected. For the past twenty years, the region has benefited from efficient long term planning and administration and its mountain farming population has increased and prospered in contrast to farming trends in other regions of Europe. Highly attractive tax incentives, cheap land, a subsidized infrastructure and excellent communications have attracted several large Japanese and German companies to the area. The region is served by the Munich-Verona railway line and an efficient motorway system. Bolzano and Trento are the region's main towns, situated in the heart of the Dolomites that form the region's north-eastern border with Austria. The area is visited by large numbers of tourists in search of mountain holidays and winter sports, and Cortina d'Ampezzo is one of the most popular ski resorts in Europe. The area also produces some excellent wines.

Emilia-Romagna

The name Emilia-Romagna derives from the ancient Roman road to Rome, Via Emilia, and Romana, a former Papal State. The northern part of the region is flat and agricultural, while the south reaches into the foothills of the Apennine Mountains. Attractive towns and the rich historic, cultural and gastronomic heritage of this prosperous region make it an attractive place to live and work. Although the cost of living is high, property prices have remained quite reasonable. In the last fifty years, the region's industrial importance has mushroomed and the economy has been transferring itself from an agricultural base to a modern industrialized one. The area has an unemployment rate of only 3·8% (the national average is around 12%) and actually faces a shortage of labour. The areas around Modena and Bologna accommodate, among other things, light industry, food processing and ceramics. Ravenna is an important port and home to the Ferruzi

Group who have a wide range of interests including oil seed, cement and sugar production as well as a controlling interest in Montedison, one of Italy's largest chemical companies. Some 45,000 small businesses, tourism, the manufacture of farm machinery and luxury sports cars (the town is the home of Ferrari, Bugatti, Maserati and de Tomaso) and other forms of industry are estimated to have given Modena the highest per capita income in Italy. The region as a whole has the second highest per capita income in Italy. Modena is also the hometown of the world famous tenor, Luciano Pavarotti. Forli has an important fruit- and vegetable-processing industry while Bologna is famous for its electronics, packaging and mechanical industries. Bologna, the seat of Europe's oldest university, is also renowned for its gastronomy – the creation and cooking of pasta has been elevated to an art form here.

Veneto

(For more details on Venice see page 113)

The Veneto region probably contains more historic, artistic and cultural treasures than any other region in Europe. Venice is the main city, but Verona, Vicenza and Padua are also of great historic and cultural importance. Commercial and maritime power meant that Venice was already a powerful state by the year 1000 and the city was the main conduit for trade between Europe and the Orient. During the 15th century, the supremacy of Venice was rivalled by Genoa, but in a series of sea battles, Venice was the victor. With the conquests of Brescia and Bergamo, the State reached the limits of its expansion on land, while on the sea, her supremacy was threatened by the fall of Constantinople in 1453. During the 16th century, Venice trod a delicate path in European affairs between France and the Hapsburgs and interference from the Popes. The Turks were also trying to usurp the Venetian trading interests and all this combined to herald a decline in Venice's fortunes and left an opening for Genoa to regain some of her lost ground. In 1797 as part of Napoleon Bonaparte's new

Europe, Venice became part of the Austrian Empire. But in 1804, after Napoleon had crowned himself King of Italy, Venice (and Lombardy) joined the new Kingdom of Italy. After the defeat of Napoleon, the region once more regained its independence until, after another short period under Austrian control, Venice became part of the newly unified Kingdom of Italy in 1861. The Veneto of is one of Italy's most successful business regions with small and medium sized companies producing high quality goods such as shoes, clothes, spectacle frames, medical equipment and mechanical components. Among the many major companies who have made their home in this region are the clothing giants Benetton, Stefanel and Carrera jeans. Other commercial activities include printing and publishing, natural stone, wine, cakes and foods, banking, light and heavy engineering, advertising, business consultancy and research. Verona is the area's commercial hub and is centrally located on main railway lines (Munich–Verona) and motorway systems providing excellent communications with central Europe. The city is home to pharmaceutical, transport, engineering and publishing industries and boasts Italy's third largest exhibition centre. Vicenza is known for tanning of leather goods, textiles, industrial jewellery and ceramics as well as steel and mechanical engineering. Marzotto, the largest wool producer in Europe, has its headquarters in Vicenza. Padua has mechanical engineering, as well as finance and services industries. Treviso has some mechanical engineering but specializes in textiles, sportswear and ceramics. Venice has a long and historic tradition of glass production and fishing and today has some heavy industry as well. The city has a tiny permanent population of only 75,000 but annual visitors to the city number more than 23m. and tourism is an important source of income, not just for Venice but for the whole region.

Friuli-Veneto

In the 19th century the region was linked with the Hapsburgs, and later, in the aftermath of World War II, it was divided between Italy and

Yugoslavia. The last remaining territorial dispute between the two countries was not resolved until 1970. The region is more ethnically mixed and has more eastern influences than other more typical Italian regions and Trieste, the national capital, projects far into Slovenia. Today, the region has developed a programme of tax and financial incentives to attract investors but owing to the region's somewhat isolated geographical and political position, foreign and Italian companies have been relatively slow to respond. Today, however, the region is starting to boom, with one of its main advantages being its proximity to the rapidly changing economies of Eastern Europe. The industrial area of Porto Marghera in the Venetian Lagoon was established in the 1920s and there is shipbuilding along the coast towards Trieste. As well as traditional heavy industry, smaller enterprises producing consumer goods have sprung up. Belluno has spectacle-making while Pordenone (the main town of the province) is a dynamic cultural and economic centre as well as being home to a large Zanussi base. Pordenone also plays host to an annual international business fair and many other events based on sectors of local commerce and industry – machine tools, horticulture, food and catering, electronics, hi-fi, optical equipment and design. The number of agricultural workers in the region is decreasing at a faster rate than the national average while the number of industrial workers is increasing proportionally faster.

Upper Centre

Regions: Tuscany, Umbria, Marche
Main Cities: Pisa, Florence, Siena, Orvieto, Perugia, Urbino

Toscana (Tuscany)

(For more details on Florence see page 119)
Tuscany was originally a Marquisite under Matilda of Tuscany, and its wealth stems from the woollen and cloth industries that were thriving during the 13th and 14th centuries. Florence was the political, cultural

and artistic centre of the Renaissance attracting artists, musicians and writers from all over Europe. Florence existed as a Republic under the Medicis, becoming a kingdom when Cosimo de Medici made himself Grand Duke of Tuscany in 1570. Later, in the 18th century, Tuscany became part of Austria when the Risorgimento was under way and Florence had a short period under Napoleonic French rule before becoming part of the unified Kingdom of Italy. Tuscany has about 57% of the population of the three regions of the Upper Centre and relies heavily on tourism (as well as the millions of tourist that flock to the area, there are approximately 8,000 British residents and many other foreigners with holiday homes). The Italian population has declined somewhat as the area has been suffering from economic depression in recent years. Prato, near to Florence, is the heart of the largest textile area in Italy incorporating more than a thousand companies. Nearby Santa Croce sull'Arno houses Italy's biggest tanning industry which provides the raw materials for the local shoe and leather industry. Pisa and Lucca are home to a large paper making industry while Empoli is known for its glass and pottery production. Livorno is a major city port and Italy's largest container port. Other industries in Tuscany include steel, electronics, furniture, and medical equipment. Olive oil is produced throughout the region and Carerra houses the quarries that have produced world famous marbles used by sculptors for hundreds of years. The part of Tuscany most popular with the British residents and holidaymakers has been dubbed Chianti-shire, a name coined from one of the most famous of Italians wines – Chianti.

Umbria

Umbria is rapidly challenging Tuscany as the most popular holiday destination for foreign tourists in the region despite the absence of good communications – the nearest international airports are Rome to the south and Pisa to the north. For the moment, prices are still about half of those in Tuscany although, since the area is within relatively easy reach of Rome (Perugia is three hours from Rome by car), it is becoming a popular weekend spot for Romans and this is likely to bump up the prices. Umbria is a landlocked province on a seismic fault line that runs down the centre of Italy. The Province contains numerous historic and cultural towns, among them Assisi, a mecca for millions of annual pilgrims, which was badly damaged by a recent earthquake. Umbria has a Foreigners' University based in Perugia that attracts students from all over the world to take courses in the Italian culture, language and art history. The region is mainly agricultural although there are important steel works at Terni and a ceramics factory near Perugia.

Le Marche

At the centre of the Marche region lies Urbino, the renaissance court of Frederico di Montefeltro who made his city one of the most aristocratic and civilized courts in Europe. Today, Marche is a varied region with a remote and beautiful isolated mountainous hinterland and a coastline whose resort towns, such as Rimini and Riccioni, are popular summer playgrounds for foreign tourists as well as Italians from the industrial north. Property prices along the coast are astronomically high because of the high demand for summer holiday homes but elsewhere the prices have stayed low as, apart from the coastal resorts, the province is almost unknown outside Italy. Like Umbria, Marche is predominantly agricultural although the Merloni Group (an enormous producer of white goods) is based in the area.

Lower Centre and Sardinia

Regions: Lazio (Latium), Abruzzo, Molise and Sardinia
Main Cities: Rome, L'Aquila, Isernia

Lazio

The region of Lazio encompasses Rome. (*See also Rome profile on page 74*)

21 April 753 BC is generally accepted as the date of the foundation of Rome and archaeological discoveries have confirmed a settlement on the Palatinate dating from that period. However it is the legend of Romulus and Remus, twin sons of Rhea Silva and the Roman God of War, Mars, that most people like to regard as the real foundation of the city. Rome is known as the Eternal City. For centuries, Rome has occupied a central place at the heart of the civilized world. In 1861, when a newly unified Italy was declared a kingdom under King Vittorio Emanuele II, Rome was the automatic choice of capital for the new nation. Other Italian cities had more of a claim to this status. Milan, Turin and Naples had all been administrative centres or capitals for centuries. But Rome had the advantage of being at the very centre of the peninsula and, with the Vatican City State, it was the symbolic, historic and cultural centre of the country. The cost of building up the city was ruinous but continued until the start of World War II. In the run up to 2000, Rome is once more under scaffolding for a huge programme of extensive renovation. Rome houses all the Italian state government administrative offices and over the years, as the bureaucracy has ballooned, it has created an enormous amount of employment for state employees, many of whom have come to Rome from the poorer regions of the south. Rome also acts as headquarters for all the major Italian banks, the majority of public utilities, and state agencies (for example, RAI, the state Italian television company, ENEL, the National Electricity Board, CNR, the National Research Council, the Italian state railways and the Southern Italian Economic Development Board). Rome is primarily concerned with the services industries but a number of neighbouring towns have become centres of intense industrial activity. Among them, Frosinone, Palatina, Aprilla, Pomezia, Civita Castellana and Rieti specialize in the production of electronics, telecommunications, light engineering, pharmaceuticals and chemicals. The three regions of Lazio, Abruzzo and Molise together account for 11% of GNP and 12·1% of the total national expenditure on goods and services (with Lazio alone accounting for over 10%).

Sardinia

Sardinia is the second largest island in the Mediterranean after Sicily. The island was inhabited by the Nuraghic people around 2000 BC and although little is known about their culture, the island is dotted with their distinctive cone shaped dwellings and fortresses. The island was invaded first by the Phoenicians, then the Carthaginians and finally settled by the Romans who turned the island into a peaceful cultural colony. Local government and decentralisation followed until the 14th century when Sardinia was conquered by the Pisans, the Aragonese and Spanish. In the 19th century, Vittorio Emanuele II began his campaign to unify Italy from this island and finally in 1848, Sardinia regained some degree of autonomous administration.

As recently as 20 years ago, most of the land in Sardinia was owned by Padroni (absentee landlords) and operated on a system of worker's patronage. The founder of the Communist party in Italy, Antonio Gramsci, and its late secretary general, Enrico Berlinguer, were both Sardinians and the party gained strength in the island by offering to liberate the agricultural workers from what they saw as the evils of 'serfdom'. Partly as a result, much of the agricultural land is today owned by the people who work on it, barren though it is. In the last 20 years, exclusive resorts have sprung up along the coastline (one of the most famous being the Costa Smeralda in the north-east) and efforts are being made to develop the interior of the island as a tourist resort. The islanders have their own language – Sardo (a mixture of Italian, Spanish, Latin, and Punic) – and there is even a small community that speaks a 15th century version of Catalan. The island is almost entirely given over to subsistence farming with tourism as the main source of income.

South

Regions: Campania, Apulia (Puglia), Basilicata, Calabria
Main Cities: Naples, Amalfi, Lecce, Bari, Brindisi, Reggio

Campania

(For more details on Naples see page 100)

Campania was called Campania Felix (Happy Country) by the Romans, who built palatial villas along the Bay of Naples. The city of Naples was first a Greek settlement and then a pleasure resort for the Romans, and the whole area is rich with myth and legends. In ancient times, it was believed that sirens lured sailors to their death off Sorrento, that the islands of the Bay of Naples were inhabited by mermaids and that Lake Avernus was the entrance to the underworld. Odysseus (Ulysses), Aeneas and other mythical heroes of the ancient world have left their legendary marks on the region. A little south of Naples, Pompeii provides the visitor with a vivid impression of life in the province in 79 AD when life was brought to an abrupt halt by a volcanic eruption and the entire city was petrified in volcanic rock. In 1503, Naples and the kingdom of Sicily were absorbed into Spain and were ruled by viceroys. Naples flourished artistically and much of the architectural splendour is owed to the Spanish rulers of this period. The Spanish Bourbons re-established Naples as a capital of the Kingdom of the Two Sicilies in 1734. During the 18th century, Naples was a favourite of the British who counted it as an essential stage on the 'Grand Tour'. Apart from a brief Napoleonic interlude from 1806 to 1815, the Bourbons ruled the region until the arrival of Garibaldi and the Kingdom of Italy in 1861. Naples was a strong contender to be the new capital city of Italy and has remained the capital of the south (or Mezzogiorno), as Milan is the capital of the north. The Roman palaces along the Bay of Naples have long since been replaced by factories and docks. Campania's main industries are food processing, canning, tanning, leather goods, ship building and steel, railway rolling stock and chemicals. Aerospace, electronics, telecommunications and motor vehicles are among the newer industries that have attracted the greatest amount of investment from major international companies. The area's hinterland remains relatively undeveloped and although the four regions that make up the South have a total working population of 4m., they also have an unemployment rate of around 20%. Tourism is very important to the area and the islands in the Bay of Naples (Ischia, Capri and Procida) have some of the highest property prices in Italy. The main coastal areas away from the industrial Neapolitan suburbs have some attractive resorts, among them Sorrento, Amalfi, Positano and Ravello. These have been extremely popular with foreign and domestic visitors for two centuries.

Apulia (Puglia)

Apulia is bordered by two coastlines, the coast of the Adriatic Sea to the east and the Ionic Sea to the south (also known as the Gulf of Taranto). Through the centuries, the region's key maritime position has made it a desirable target for colonizers and traders. The ancient Greeks founded a string of settlements along the Ionian coast including Taranto. Brindisi marks the end of the Appian Way and the Normans, who inhabited the region in the 11th century, left behind a magnificent heritage of Romanesque churches and cathedrals. In the 16th century, the Spanish built 'Trulli' (conical, circular, dry-stone built houses) in the area between Bari and Taranto and the Holy Roman Emperor, Frederick II, left behind castles in the province of Foggia. Lecce, settled by the Spanish, is known as the Florence of Baroque. The regional capital is Bari, and the highest proportion of the population of the region is concentrated in and around the city. The city and its surrounding areas have a high concentration of energetic small industries and a 'Feria del Lavante' is held there every year. Taranto is a major steel producing area with a number of ancillary businesses, although in recent years steel production has had to be cut in order to comply with European Union directives. Foggia is the centre for agricultural production. The main crops are hard wheat, wine, olives and olive oil, chestnuts, hazelnuts, tomatoes, vegetables and fruit (citrus fruits and kiwi in particular). Agriculture still accounts for 18% of the local gross product although the number of people directly engaged in agriculture is on the wane and land holdings remain relatively small. Despite efforts by the Italian government to redress the balance, the gap between the lower per capita income of the south and the higher one in the north is widening. There is no lack of ready money in the south, however, and there is a large consumer market for retail (even luxury) items – there are approximately 4,000 wholesalers and 99,000 retailers in Campania. The area is rich in natural beauty. The upper part of the region, graced with wooded hills and stunning views across the Adriatic, is considered the most attractive part of the area. The islands 25 miles off Gargano were once the 'Devil's Island' of Italy but now attract tourists (more than 100,000 people visited the islands in Aug. 1998) rather than prisoners. The ports of Otranto and Brindisi have regular ferry sailings to Greece and Yugoslavia.

Basilicata (Lucania) and Calabria
Calabria and Basilicata contain 20% of the southern region's population although they are still relatively undeveloped. In the 1950s the Italian government set up the Cassa del Mezzogiorno, a regional development fund to help develop the Southern provinces (the Mezzogiorno). But despite its efforts to bring industrial development to the region, there is still very little industry in these two areas and their economies depend largely on agriculture and tourism. Enormous amounts of government money have been poured into the area to fund irrigation schemes, improve the infrastructure and establish modern communications. After years of financial management problems in the area, the EU Regional Investment Fund took over the responsibility for funding the Mezzogiorno. To add to the existing economic problems, the area has been severely depopulated with workers migrating north in search of better-paid work. Calabria forms the 'toe' at the south western tip of the Italian peninsula and its beautiful coastline draws a regular number of tourists every

year in summer. The cities in Calabria, in particular Reggio Calabria and Crotone, have a reputation for kidnapping (for the ransom money rather than political gain) and for organized crime, usually affecting the local professional classes, rather than the foreign visitor. The region's income is mainly from agriculture and, like Campania, the main crops are hard wheat, wine, olive oil, nuts, fruits and vegetables. Calabria has 42,000 retailers and 4,500 wholesalers. Basilicata has 11,000 retailers and 700 wholesalers.

Sicily

Main cities: Palermo, Syracuse, Catania, Messina, Agrigento
(For more details on Palermo see page 107)
Sicily's unique historic and ethnic heritage explains its status as a 'Regioni a Statuto Speciale', which means that it enjoys a greater degree of autonomy than most of the other twenty regions of Italy. The earliest settlers on Sicily were believed to be the Sicanians, Elymians and Siculians who came from various points around the Mediterranean. These were followed by the Phoenicians and then the Greeks who started to colonize the island in the 8th century BC. The cities of Syracuse, Catania, Messina and Agrigento, founded by the Greeks, still dominate the island. By 210 BC, Sicily was under Roman control. Power then passed to Byzantium and then to the Arabs who settled there in 903 AD. The Norman conquest came in 1060 when Roger I captured Messina. Control of Sicily passed to the house of Hohenstaufen and the Swabians under Frederick II (the Holy Roman Emperor who was known as 'Stupor Mundi' or 'Wonder of the World'). Misrule by the French during the 13th century led to an uprising known as the Sicilian Vespers in 1281 and the island passed to the Spanish Aragon family and then, in 1503, to the Spanish Crown. Savoy and Austria each ruled the island briefly and in the 18th century the Bourbons of Naples brought the island under Spanish control. In 1860, Garibaldi landed at Marsala with his 'One Thousand' and

peninsula showed that man's nomadic days were over, and at the beginning of the Bronze Age Italy housed several Italic tribes – among them the Ligurians, Veneti, the Apulians, the Siculi, the Sardi and many others. Although opinions differ as to whether the Etruscans were native to Italy or whether they migrated from the Asian coast of the Aegean Sea, it is generally accepted that they were established in Italy by around 1200 BC. Theirs was a highly civilized society that flourished between the Arno and Tiber valleys with other important settlements in Campania, Lazio and the Po valley. The Etruscans were primarily navigators and travellers competing for the valuable trading routes and markets with the Phoenicians and Greeks. Rather like the Egyptians before them, the Estruscans were buried with everything they might need in the afterlife and their painted tombs (especially those in Tarquinia) leave an accurate picture of how they lived. During the 8th century BC, the Greeks had begun to settle in southern Italy and presented a serious challenge to Etruscan domination of sea trade routes. Greek settlements were established along the southern coast, on the island of Ischia in the Bay of Naples and in Sicily where the Corinthians founded the city of Syracuse. These colonies were known as Magna Graecia and flourished for about 6 centuries. The ruins of Doric temples at Paestum in the south of Italy and in Agrigento, Selinunte and Segesta in Sicily as well as the Greek theatre in Syracuse give an idea of the magnificence of their civilization. Magna Graecia eventually succumbed to the growing power of Rome where the impact of the Hellenic culture had already been felt.

According to legend, Rome was founded on 21 April 753 BC by Romulus (a descendant of Aeneas, a Trojan) who, after killing his twin brother, Remus, declared himself the first King of Rome. The Etruscan dynasty of Tarquins gained control in 616 BC and expanded Roman agriculture and trade to rival the Greeks. The Romans overthrew the Tarquins in 510 BC and the first Roman Republic was born.

With the birth of the first Republic of Rome came the establishment of the 'Roman Code', a collection of basic principles of political philosophy that enshrined the sovereign rights of Roman citizens and constituted one of the most important Roman contributions to civilisation. The initials SPQR (Senatus and Populus Que Romanus – The Senate and People of Rome) can still be seen, not only on the ancient monuments but stamped on municipal property in Rome to this day. The early Roman Senate was dominated by a few patrician families who with the 'Equites' (the highest class of non-noble rich) held a virtual monopoly of public offices.

With the exception of the Greek city-states, Italy was unified by the Romans who, having almost conquered the Italian peninsula, set their sights on the Mediterranean, which was still controlled by Carthage. Between 264 BC and 146 BC, Carthage and Rome fought three wars (The Punic Wars) for supremacy of the valuable trade routes of the Mediterranean. At the start, Carthage was more powerful than Rome with a colonial Empire that stretched as far as Morocco and included Sicily, Corsica, Sardinia and parts of Spain. Rome had never fought a maritime war, and it was only when a Carthaginian war ship was washed up on the shore that the Romans had a design for constructing a fleet of their own. In 218 BC the second Punic War started when Hannibal crossed the Alps with his elephants and marched south, defeating the Romans in one bloody battle after another all the way through Italy. He crossed over to Zama in North Africa where he was finally defeated by Scipio in 202 BC. By the end of the third Punic War in 146 BC, the destruction of Carthage and with it her civilisation and culture was total and Macedonian Greece had been added to Rome's provinces. Rome incorporated Spain into her colonies and became the dominant power in the Mediterranean. This dominance of trade routes led to great riches for Rome and the ensuing corruption among the upper ruling classes gave rise to social unrest. Sulla, a patrician General, marched on Rome in 82 BC, took the city in a bloody coup and instituted a new constitution and reforms. Nine years later Spartacus, an escaped slave, led 70,000 of his fellow slaves in a violent rampage throughout the length and breadth of the peninsula. Out of the ensuing chaos, Julius Caesar emerged as leader. He had already conquered Gaul and declared southern Britain a part of Rome in 54 BC, and although his flagrant disregard for the authority of the Senate had led to his legions being disbanded he was immensely popular and returned to Rome a hero. His great strength and charisma led to his assassination by jealous members of the Senate on the Ides of March 44 BC. After his death, various rival successors fought to gain control, including Anthony, Cleopatra and Brutus. But it was Caesar's nephew Octavian, having defeated Mark Anthony in 31 BC, who in 27 BC was crowned first Emperor of Rome, assuming the title Augustus.

Augustus reigned for 45 years. With the aid of a professional army and an imperial bureaucracy he kept peace at home while extending the Roman Empire and disseminating her laws and civic culture abroad. The arts thrived with writers, dramatists and philosophers like Cicero, Plautus, Terence, Virgil, Horace and Ovid developing Latin into an expressive and poetic language that would later help shape the Romance languages of modern Europe (French, Spanish, Portuguese, Italian, Romanian, etc.). This golden age of Rome (known as 'Pax Romana' or 200 years of peace) continues to influence modern European thought and literature to the present day. In 100 BC, Rome itself had more than 1·5m. inhabitants and the Roman Empire was a unified diversity of many different races and creeds. It had more than 100,000 km of paved roads, a complex of sophisticated aqueducts, an efficient army and administrative system supporting a postal service and even a telegraphic system which used a complicated system of light signals.

In 14 AD Augustus was succeeded by his stepson, Tiberius, who ruled in an era that was to see the rise of Christianity. Successive

Emperors tried to suppress this new religion spread by the followers of Christ who travelled as far afield as Northumberland in the north of Britain and Egypt in North Africa, and from Portugal to Syria. The deranged and corrupt Emperor Nero who came to power in 54 AD initiated violent persecution of the Christians and, it is often claimed, caused Rome to burn to the ground. His reign brought the Julio-Claudian dynasty to an end and, after a period of instability, Vespasian, the son of a provincial civil servant, took the throne and began some of the most ambitious building projects the Empire had seen. He started the Coliseum (which was completed by his son Titus) and the Arco di Tito (where the Via Sacra joins the Forum).

In 98 AD, Trajan was appointed Emperor by the Senate. Beginning a century of successful rule by the Antonine dynasty, he expanded the Empire with the successful conquests of Dacia (Romania), Mesopotamia, Persia, Syria and Armenia. By the end of his reign the Roman Empire stretched from present-day Kuwait to Britain, from the Caspian Sea to Morocco and Portugal, and from North Africa to the Danube and Romania. Trajan rebuilt Claudius' harbour at Ostia (still perfectly preserved), and the amphitheatre at Verona. Under his direction, the architect Appollodorus of Damascus built the kilometre long bridge over the Danube and designed Trajan's Forum in Rome. A column decorated with hundreds of carvings depicting Trajan's Dacian campaign later served as his tomb and remains standing to this day. Trajan's successor, Hadrian, continued with this programme of huge constructions, adding the Villa Adriana at Tivoli near Rome and Hadrian's Wall in Britain to Rome's architectural legacy. After his death in 138 AD, his tomb was converted into the fortress of Castel Sant'Angelo on the banks of the Tiber.

During the 2nd century AD, a plague swept through Europe and, under pressure from Teutonic tribes along the Danube and as a result of the increasingly strong influence of the Eastern religions, Rome began to lose control over her enormous Empire. In 306, Constantine became Emperor and after he converted to Christianity in 313, his 'Edict of Milan' gave official recognition to Christianity, thus bringing to an end two centuries of religious persecution and establishing Rome as the new headquarters of the Christian religion. A new building programme of Christian cathedrals and churches began throughout the peninsula. At the same time, Constantine decided to cultivate the wealthy eastern regions of the Empire and, in 324, he moved his capital to Constantinople (now Istanbul) on the northern shore of the Bosphorus Sea in Byzantium. The demise of the Roman Empire continued when, after the death of Constantine, two brothers, Valens and Valentian, divided the Empire down the middle from north to south. The eastern half became separated from Rome and gradually developed into the Byzantine Empire, the most powerful Mediterranean state through the middle ages until it was captured by the Turks in 1453.

The western half of the Roman Empire, having embraced Christianity as the state religion, was coming under repeated attacks from Barbarians. The Germanic Vandals had cut off Rome's corn supplies from North Africa, and the Visigoths, a Teutonic tribe, controlled the northern Mediterranean coast and northern Italy. In 452, Attila the Hun, leader of a tribe from the steppes of central Asia, invaded and forced the people of north-eastern Italy into a haven that came to be known as Venice. Rome was captured and sacked in 455 by the Vandals and in 476 a Germanic mercenary captain called Odovacar deposed Romulus Augustus, the last of the Western Roman Emperors. This date is generally accepted as the end of the Roman Empire.

· In 493 Odovacar was succeeded by Theodoric, an Ostrogoth who had spent time as a hostage in Constantinople and who had acquired a taste for Roman culture. Theodoric ruled from Ravenna and by the time he died in 527 he had managed to restore peace and harmony to Italy. On his death, Italy was re-conquered by an Emperor of the

Eastern Roman Empire, Justinian, who together with his wife Theodora laid the foundations of the Byzantine period. Although the Lombards drove back the Justinian conquest, Byzantine Emperors managed to retain control of parts of southern Italy until the 11th century.

In the middle of the 5th century, Attila the Hun had been persuaded not to attack Rome by Pope Leo I (known as 'The Great'). This and a document known as the 'Donation of Constantine' secured the Western Roman Empire for the Catholic Church. In 590, Gregory I became Pope and set about an extensive programme of reforms including improved conditions for slaves and the distribution of free bread in Rome. He oversaw the Christianization of Britain, repaired Italy's network of aqueducts and created the foundations for future centuries of Catholic services and rituals and church administrative systems.

The invasion of Italy by the Lombards began before Gregory became Pope and, although they eventually penetrated as far south as Spoleto and Benevento, they were unable to take Rome. They set-tled around Milan, Pavia and Brescia and, like so many other invaders of the peninsula, they virtually abandoned their own language and customs in favour of the local culture. However they were sufficiently threatening to cause the Pope to invite the Franks under King Pepin to invade. In 756 the Franks overthrew the Lombards and established the Papal States (which survived until 1870). Pepin took the 'Donation of Constantine' as his example and issued his own 'Donation of Pepin' which gave the land still controlled by the Byzantine Empire to Pope Stephen II, proclaiming him and future Popes the heirs of the Roman Emperors. Pepin's son, Charlemagne, succeeded him and was crowned Emperor on Christmas Day 800 by Pope Leo III in St. Peter's Basilica in Rome. Thus the concept of the 'Holy Roman Empire' was born which broke the tie between Rome and Byzantium once and for all. The seat of European political power moved north of the Alps where it would remain for more than 1,000 years.

After Charlemagne's death it proved impossible to keep the enormous Empire together. In the period of anarchy which followed, many small independent rival states were established while in Rome the aristocratic families fought ruthlessly over the Papacy and the imperial crown. Meanwhile, southern Italy was prospering under Moslem rule. By 831, Moslem Arabs had invaded Sicily and made Palermo their capital. Syracuse fell to them in 878. They created a Greek style civilisation with Moslem philosophers, physicians, astronomers, mathematicians and geographers. Cotton, sugar cane and citrus fruits appeared for the first time in Italy and taxes were lowered. Hundreds of Mosques were built and all over the region centres of academic and medical learning sprang up and thrived. Southern Italy lived harmoniously under Arab influence for more than 200 years but further north things were not so settled. After the collapse of the Carolingian Empire, warfare broke out between local rulers forcing many people to take refuge in fortified hill towns. In 962, Otto I, a Saxon, was crowned Holy Roman Emperor, the first of a succession of Germanic Emperors that was to continue until 1806.

At the beginning of the 11th century, the Normans began to arrive in great numbers in southern Italy where they had originally been recruited to fight the Arabs. Establishing themselves successfully in Apulia and Calabria, they assimilated much of the eastern culture, coexisting peacefully with the Arabs. The architecture of churches and cathedrals built during this period shows the merging of the two cultural and religious influences in the open rounded arches and large interior spaces, often decorated with elaborate mosaics. Meanwhile, the delicate relationship between the Holy Roman Empire based in the north of Europe and the Papacy in the south was maintained by a common desire to recapture the Holy Land from the Moslems. Crusades were launched, mostly from the northern states, but achieved little. Germanic claims to the southern territories grew and after Frederick I (known as Barbarossa) was crowned Holy

Roman Emperor in 1155, he married off his son Henry to the heir to the Norman throne in Sicily thus ensuring the success of the Germanic claim. Frederick II, who was Frederick Barbarossa's grandson, came to the throne of Southern Italy in 1220. He was known as 'Stupor Mundi' ('Wonder of the World') and was an enlightened and tolerant ruler. Although an accomplished warrior, he valued scholarship and greatly admired the Arab culture. He allowed both Moslems and Jews freedom to follow their own religions. An ardent student of philosophy, he developed a legal framework and gave Italy some of its earliest poetry. He founded the University of Naples in 1224 with the intention of producing a generation of administrators for his kingdom and moved the court of the Holy Roman Empire to the newly built octagonal masterpiece, Castel del Monte, in Apulia.

During this period, a new rich middle class emerged but with the seat of government so far south, some of the northern cities began to free themselves from feudal control and set themselves up as autonomous states under the protection of either the Pope or the Emperor. Milan, Cremona, Bologna, Florence, Pavia, Modena, Parma and Lodi were the most important of these new states and were, for the most part, dominated by individual families who exercised governmental power in the form of 'Signorias'. These states functioned autonomously within larger regional areas: Veneto, Lombardy, Tuscany, The Papal States and the Southern Kingdom. In 1265, Charles of Anjou (a Frenchman who had beheaded Frederick II's grandson) was crowned King of Sicily. His greatly increased taxes, especially on rich landowners, made him unpopular despite his programme of road repairs, reform of the monetary system, improvement of the ports and the opening of silver mines. In 1282, an uprising known as the Sicilian Vespers was sparked off by a French soldier assaulting a Sicilian woman. As a consequence of the opposition to the French in southern Italy, the citizens of Palermo declared themselves an independent republic while supporting the Spaniard, Peter of Aragon, as King. By 1302, the Anjou dynasty had established itself in Naples.

The Black Death (also known as La Peste), a deadly plague that swept throughout Europe towards the end of the 13th century, decimated the populations of the major cities who were already struggling with famine after long years of war. Despite this, the strength of the northern and central Italian city-states was increasing. The rival maritime republics of Venice and Genoa each had their own fleets. Venice had added the ports of Dalmatia, Greece and Cyprus to her possessions and Genoa's influence stretched as far as the Black Sea. Meanwhile, the Pope and the Church turned their crusading zeal, which had been used against the eastern infidels throughout the 13th century, against European heretics. Under the guise of saving souls, the Italian ruling families were amassing enormous wealth and property. Pope Boniface, who had been elected in 1294, came from Italian nobility and was determined to safeguard the long term interests of his own family. He claimed Papal supremacy in worldly and spiritual affairs with his Papal Bull (Unam Sanctam) in 1302. Meanwhile, a rival Papacy had appeared in Avignon where John XXII was based. Rome had lost most of her former glory and had become little more than a battleground for the Orisini and Colonna families who were engaged in a vast power struggle. The Papal claim to be temporal rulers of Rome was under threat and the Papal States began to fall apart. The period between 1305 and 1377, when seven successive Popes ruled in Avignon, became known as the 'Babylonian Captivity' (a phrase originally coined by the Roman Poet laureate, Plutarch, and later used to condemn the evils of French influence). In 1377, Pope Gregory XI returned to Rome after Cardinal Egidio d'Albornoz managed to restore the Papal States with his Egidian Constitutions. Rome was in such a ruined state that Gregory was obliged to set up his court in the Vatican which was fortified and protected by the proximity of the Castel Sant'Angelo. Gregory died a year later when the Roman

Cardinals elected one of their own, Urban VI, as his successor. Urban's unpopularity was such that the French Cardinals rebelled, electing their own Pope, Clement VII, who set up his rival claim in Avignon. Yet another rival Pope set himself in Pisa and thus began the Great Schism that would separate the Papacy from Rome for nearly half a century.

With the rise of the city-states came humanism, a secular movement that believed in the glory of human achievement and potential independent of any divine involvement. Inspired by these ideals, Italy was at the forefront of the greatest flowering of artistic and intellectual expression in history, the Renaissance. In 1418, the Great Schism was brought to an end by the Council of Constance and once again Rome began to recapture her previous glory. Throughout the 15th century, the powerful ruling families like the Medicis in Florence, the Gonzagas in Mantua and the d'Estes in Ferrara financed the creation of great works of art. Rome grew in size, power and beauty. At the height of the Renaissance, the city had 100,000 inhabitants and was once again the centre of Italian political, cultural and intellectual life. In Florence, the Signoria was taken over by a wealthy merchant, Cosimo de Medici. His nephew, Lorenzo II Magnifico, made a place for himself in history as one of the greatest patrons of the arts. He concentrated his talents in building the prestige of the city by attracting the finest artists of the day to work there. Feudal lords like Lorenzo de Medici frequently switched allegiance between the Popes and the Emperors, becoming enormously wealthy bankers and captains of adventure in the process. They competed with one another to create the finest, richest and most cultured cities. But in the latter half of the 15th century, a dissenting voice was heard in Florence. A Dominican monk, Girolamo Savonarola, preaching hell fire against what he perceived as the evils of humanist thinking, persuading the French King, Charles VIII, to overthrow the Medici family and declare a republic. Although he was eventually

excommunicated, hanged and burned at the stake, Savonarola exerted a powerful and lasting influence on Florentine politics. Florence's
time as a republic was brief though. The Emperor Charles V, who had
sacked Rome in 1527, reinstated the Medicis who went on to rule
Florence for the next 210 years.

Nor did all Italian cities thrive. In the south, the Visconti family
formed an alliance with Alfonso V of Aragon to fight the Angevins,
thus ensuring the repression of freethinking and creativity so preva-
lent in the stronger Italian cities.

By the second half of the 16th century, the Church of Rome was
obliged to respond to the rise of the Protestant movement (or
'Reformation'), inspired in Germany by Martin Luther. During what
came to be known as the Counter-Reformation, the judicial arm of the
church, the Inquisition, backed by the Catholic armies of Spain, was
used to discover and suppress heresy. The whole of Europe was sub-
jected to a sustained campaign of torture and fear that lasted for
nearly a hundred years. Spain succeeded in dominating Italy during
the second half of the 16th century but when the Emperor Charles II
(the last of the Spanish Hapsburgs) died in 1700, the War of the
Spanish Succession resulted in Italy becoming a prize to be bar-
gained over by the dominant European powers. During the early part
of the eighteenth century, Italy was mostly ruled from abroad. The
Papacy became less influential, the Jesuits were expelled from
Portugal, France and Spain and, thanks to the intermarriage between
many of the ruling houses of Europe and new trading laws, many of
the national barriers were broken down. The Age of Enlightenment, as
the 18th century came to be known, gave Italy some of its greatest
thinkers and writers and many of the most liberal and enlightened
laws and reforms of the criminal code were instigated during this
period.

In 1796, a young Corsican born French General, Napoleon
Bonaparte, invaded Italy and, despite violent resistance in Naples,

declared an Italian Republic under his personal rule and created for the first time a single political entity. The Italy as we know it today was born. Five years later, when Napoleon made himself Emperor of France, he persuaded a reluctant Pope Pius VII to come from Rome to crown him in Paris.

The Congress of Vienna, which met after the defeat of Napoleon in 1815, reinstated Italy's former rulers. Secret societies, largely made up of disillusioned middle class intellectuals, sprang up to fight for a new constitution to reunify the country. One such society was founded in 1830 by a Genoan, Giuseppe Mazzini. His Young Italy was committed to liberating the country from foreign dominance and to the establishment of a unified Italy under a republican government, a campaign that came to be known as 'Il Risorgimento'. During the 1830s and 1840s Mazzini instigated a series of unsuccessful uprisings. Mazzini was exiled and devoted the remainder of his days to drumming up support among influential European allies. By 1848 revolutionary uprisings were taking place all over Europe and the Italian Nationalist movement was gaining ground. Two supporters of the Nationalist cause, Cesare Balbo and Count Camillo Benso di Cavour, established their own newspaper in Turin and named it 'Il Risorgimento'. In 1848, they published a document – 'Statuto' – that proposed parliamentary reform for Italy which would create a two-chamber government with an upper chamber to be appointed by the Sovereign and a lower chamber to be elected by educated taxpayers. Although twenty more years of bitter fighting followed, the 'Statuto' would later become the basis of a new Italian constitution.

As nationalist feeling increased, Giuseppe Garibaldi, whose terrorist activities as a leading member of Mazzini's Young Italy had obliged him to flee to South America, returned to Italy to offer his services to King Charles Albert, who was fighting the Austrians. He was rejected and, after taking part in various unsuccessful military campaigns, among them an attempt to liberate the Venetian Republic, he backed the Italian National Society and took part in the campaign of 1859 against the Austrians. In 1860 he set sail from Genoa with 1,000 volunteers (the Red Shirts) to take Sicily and then Naples from the Bourbons. Garibaldi handed over these kingdoms to Victor Emmanuel II. This was much to the relief of Cavour who, from his position of power in the north, blocked Garibaldi's march on Rome with Piedmontese troops, fearing that Garibaldi might try and institute a rival republican government in the south. Although Italy was declared a Kingdom in 1861 under Victor Emmanuel II, the country was still not unified. Venice was in the hands of the Austrians while France held Rome. In 1866, the Italians took the Veneto from the Prussians and in 1870, Rome was recaptured from the French. The unification of Italy, first dreamt about by Machiavelli in the 16th century, had finally become a reality.

Meanwhile, further north, Cavour had been fighting diplomatic and political battles. In 1850, he was serving as Minister for Commerce, Finance and the Navy in the government of the Piedmontese Monarch, King Carlo Alberto under his Prime Minister, Massimo d'Azeglio. When Cavour's centre-left supporters formed an alliance with the centre-right followers of Urbino Rattazzi, d'Azeglio resigned and Cavour took over the post at the King's request. In an attempt to loosen the Austrian stranglehold on Piedmont, Cavour tried to form an alliance with the French Emperor, Napoleon III, but was betrayed when he signed the armistice of Villafranca, ending the Franco-Prussian war (which had been largely fought in Italy by Italians). In 1870, when the Italians retook Rome, only the Papal troops resisted the advance of the Italian army and Pope Pius IX refused to recognize the newly created Kingdom of Italy. In retaliation, the government stripped the Pope of his temporal powers.

The turn of the twentieth century saw most of European popular support fluctuating between left-wing socialist and right-wing imperialist political parties. When World War I broke out in 1914, Italy remained neutral although the State was associated with the British, French and Russians allies while the Papacy declared for Catholic Austria. In 1914, a young journalist, Benito Mussolini, started his own newspaper – Popolo d'Italia. Financed by the British, French and Russian allies, the paper acted as a propaganda instrument to promote the Allies' cause. In 1919, Mussolini founded the Italian Fascist Party whose black shirts and Roman salutes were to become the symbols of aggressive nationalism in Italy for the next two decades. In the elections of 1921, the Fascist Party won 35 of the 135 seats in the Italian parliament. A year later, Mussolini raised a militia of 40,000 'Black Shirts' and marched on Rome to 'liberate' it from the socialists. In 1922, the King asked Mussolini to form a government. His Fascist party won the elections of 1924 and Mussolini assumed the title Il Duce. By the end of 1925, Mussolini had expelled all opposition parties from parliament and gained control of the trade unions. Four years later, he signed a pact with Pope Pius XI declaring Catholicism the sole religion of Italy and recognising the Vatican as an independent state. In return, the Pope finally recognized the United Kingdom of Italy.

Meanwhile, Mussolini's aggressive foreign policy had resulted in squabbles with Greece over Corfu, and military campaigns in the Italian colony of Libya. In 1935, Italy invaded Abyssinia (now Ethiopia) and captured Addis Ababa. The newly formed League of Nations condemned this action and imposed sanctions. In the face of international isolation, Mussolini formed an alliance with the German dictator, Adolf Hitler, and in 1936, the Rome-Berlin Axis was formed. Italy entered World War II in June 1941. The Allied armies landed in Sicily in July 1943 and in the face of diminishing popular support for fascism and Hitler's refusal to assign more troops to the defence of Italy, the King led a coup against Mussolini and had him arrested. In the confused 45 days that followed, Italy exploded in a series of uprisings against the war. The King signed an armistice with the allies and declared war on Germany but Nazi troops had already overrun northern Italy. The Germans rescued Mussolini from prison and installed him as a puppet ruler. In 1945, after trying to flee the country disguised as a German soldier, Mussolini was eventually recaptured by Italian partisans and shot. His body was displayed hanging upside down in a public square in Como. After final violent struggles between the Italian Resistance and the German troops resulting in huge losses to the Italian Resistance, the allies finally broke through to liberate northern Italy in May 1945.

In the years following the end of World War II, Italy's political forces attempted to regroup. The Marshal Plan, USA's post-war aid programme, exerted considerable political and economic influence. The constitutional Monarchy was abolished in 1946 by referendum and a republic was formed with a President, elected for a seven-year term by an Electoral College, a two-chamber parliament and a separate Judiciary. The President is the Head of State and appoints the Prime Minister who is Chief Executive and responsible for appointing his own Council of Ministers. Initially the newly formed Christian Democrats (Democrazia Christiana) under Alcide de Gaspari were in power with both the Communist Party (the Partito Communista Italiano) and the Socialist Party (Partito Socialista Italiano) participating in a series of coalition governments until they were both excluded by de Gaspari in 1947. More than 300 separate political factions were struggling for power throughout the post-war era and no one government lasted longer than four years. But despite this political instability, the war-damaged Italian economy began to pick up in the early 1950s. The industrialized northern states thrived while the less industrialized south remained underdeveloped. The Cassa per il Mezzogiorno (a state fund for the South) was founded to try to redress the balance but with limited success.

In 1957, Italy became a founder member of the European Economic Community (EEC) and, as unemployment dropped and industrial productivity increased, Italy entered upon its Economic Miracle. The rapid growth of the motor industry, most notably Fiat in Turin, saw huge migrations of peasants from the south to work in the factories. By the mid-1960s, the Communist Party, which had been gradually increasing its share of the poll at each election, had more card carrying members than the Christian Democrats and was exerting considerable influence over Italian politics without actually managing to participate in Government. Social unrest was commonplace and in 1969, a series of strikes, demonstrations and riots followed on the heels of unrest elsewhere in Europe. Various terrorist groups were active including the extreme left-wing Socialist terrorist group, the Red Brigade (Brigade Rosse), founded in 1970. But the extreme right-wing neo-fascist terrorists were also in action, and in the less developed south, the Mafia, a loose coalition of crime 'families', flourished. Most of Italy's social, economic and political structures were manipulated by these unofficial organisations. In 1963, Aldo Moro, a Christian Democrat, was appointed Prime Minister (a post he held until 1968) and invited the Socialists into his government. Later on, in the 1970s, he was working towards a compromise to allow the Communists to enter government when he was captured, held hostage and finally murdered by the Red Brigade. This national outrage prompted the government to appoint Carabinieri General, Carlo Alberto dalla Chiesa, to wipe out the terrorist groups. He instituted a system of 'Pentiti' (repentants or informants) who, in return for collaboration, would receive greatly reduced prison sentences. In 1980, he was asked to expand his area of operations to include the Mafia only to be assassinated in Palermo a few months later. Throughout the 1970s, Italy experienced radical social and political change. The country was divided into regional administrative areas with their own elected governments. Divorce became legal, women's rights were expanded (Italian women only achieved full suffrage after World War II) and abortion was legalized. In 1983 the, by now, minority Christian

Democratic government was forced to hand over the Prime Ministership to the Socialists and Bettino Craxi became the longest serving prime minister since de Gaspari.

By now, Italy was well on its way to becoming one of the world's leading economic powers, but the 1990s brought fresh crises in both the economic and political arenas. Unemployment and inflation rose sharply which, combined with a huge national debt and very unstable lira, led to economic instability. On the political front, the Communist Party split with the hard-liners forming the Rifondazione Communista, led by Fausto Bernotti, while the more moderate members set up the Partito Democratico della Sinistra (Democratric Party of the Left) led, from 1994, by Massimo d'Alema. In early 1992, the arrest of a Socialist Party worker on charges of accepting bribes in exchange for public works contracts sparked off the largest political corruption scandal ever to hit Italy. Investigations into 'Tangentopoli' (a journalistic term coined to mean 'kick-back city'), instigated under a Milanese magistrate, Antonio di Pietro, snowballed to implicate thousands of politicians, public officials and businessmen from the most junior to the very highest levels of government. The former Prime Minster, Bettino Craxi, was forced to resign as party secretary after he was served with five notifications that he was under investigation for bribery. He fled to his villa in Tunisia where he remains to this day. The Italian people were so disillusioned with their government that in the post-scandal elections, the Christian Democrat share of the vote dropped by 5% and a new political voice began to be heard. The Lega Nord (the Northern League), under Umberto Bossi, took 7% of the vote on an anti-corruption, federalist platform. Oscar Luigi Scalfaro was elected president on a promise to set about reforming electoral laws and clearing up the 'Tangentopoli' scandal. Investigations into corruption continue, despite overt threats and reprisals from the Mafia. Craxi has been convicted in absentia while Giulio Andreotti, who was Prime Minister three times between 1972

and 1992 and who is considered one of Italy's leading post-war
politicians, was brought to trial in 1995 on charges of having dealings
with the Sicilian Mafia. It is thought that recent bomb attacks in Milan,
Florence and Rome killing several people and damaging works of
art are part of the Mafia's violent response to the clampdowns on
corruption.

During the early 1990s, Italy's political structure was seriously
undermined. The two main parties, the Christian Democrats and the
Socialists, were in chaos and in the 1994 elections, a new right-wing
coalition was elected. Called the Polo della Liberta (Freedom
Alliance), its members included the neo-fascist Alleanza Nazionale
(National Alliance) and the federalist Northern League. The leader of
this new coalition, Silvio Berlusconi, a multi-millionaire publishing
tycoon and a newcomer to politics, was appointed Prime Minister.
Berlusconi lost his majority when the Northern League withdrew after
only nine months. Under mounting criticism for his failure to disasso-
ciate himself from his business interests and after receiving a vote of
no confidence, he was forced to resign. After leaving the Freedom
Alliance, The Northern League became more fanatical, advocating
a 'Northern Republic of Padania', a separation of the rich northern
states from the poorer southern ones (a policy unlikely to receive
countrywide support). The 1996 elections brought yet another coalition to power, the centre-left 'Olive Tree' (l'Ulivo) with Romano Prodi as
Prime Minister. This professor of economics from Bologna aimed to
balance the budget and create a stable political environment. He
gained his first objective with a succession of economic measures
that prepared the way for Italy's entry into EMU. Constitutional change
proved to be harder to achieve (see page 128).

CHRONOLOGY

Early Roman History

BC

753   Legendary Foundation of Rome by Romulus.

616   Royal Dynasty of the Tarquins – power divided between king, senate (drawn from the patrician families) and comitia (representing non-patrician rich families).

509–510   The Romans overthrow the Tarquins and establish the Republic of Rome.

390   The Gauls invade Italy but are repulsed by Camillus.

264–241   First Punic War. Romans take Sicily from the Carthaginians.

218–201   Second Punic War. Hannibal crosses the Alps, marches south defeating the Romans and is halted at Capua.

204   Hannibal returns to Carthage. The Roman commander Scipio lands in Africa from Spain.

202   Scipio defeats Hannibal at Zarma.

149–146   Third Punic War. Rome conquers and destroys Carthage. Greek Macedonia becomes a Roman province.

133   Rome occupies Spain. End of Mediterranean campaigns.

118   The Romans invade Gaul.

88–79   Sulla marches on Rome and establishes a dictatorship with a new constitution.

70   Pompey and Crassus appointed consuls of Rome.

60   Rome under rule of the first triumvirate (Pompey, Crassus, Julius Caesar).

59   Julius Caesar assumes full power.

58–51   Gallic War takes place.

54   Julius Caesar declares Britain a part of Roman Empire.

49   Julius Caesar crosses the Rubicon and drives Pompey out of Rome.

49–45   Caesar defeats Pompey in Spain, Greece and Egypt.

44   Julius Caesar appointed dictator for life but assassinated on
15 March.

43   Second Triumvirate rules Rome (Octavius, Anthony, Lepidus).

41–30   Anthony, defeated by Octavius at Actium, commits
suicide.

27   Octavius becomes Augustus Caesar.

The Early Empire

1st century AD

14   Death of Augustus Caesar.

14–37   Reign of Tiberius. Start of 200 years of 'Pax Romana' –
flowering of literature and the arts. Roman Empire expands.

54–68   Reign of Nero. Persecution of early Christians.

68   Death of Nero.

69–96   Flavian Dynasty (Vespian, Titus, Domitian).

98   Trajan appointed Emperor by the Senate. Further expansion
(Roman Empire covers most of Europe and the Middle East).

2nd century

117   Hadrian succeeds Trajan. Massive building programme
commences (Hadrian's Wall in Britain, the Forum in Rome etc.).

138–193   Death of Hadrian. Plague sweeps through Europe.
Pressure from Teutonic tribes in the north. Empire begins to
disintegrate.

3rd century

193–275   Severus Dynasty.

253–268   Military anarchy descends. Roman Legions hold
power.

The Later Empire

4th century

284–305   Reign of Dioceletian. Persecution of the Christians
(Age of Martyrs).

306   Constantine becomes Emperor.

313   Edict of Milan gives Christians freedom to practise their religion.

324   Constantine moves capital of Roman Empire to Constantinople.

337   Death of Constantine.

379–395   Reign of Theodosius the Great (the Christian Emperor).

395   Empire divided into Eastern Empire and Western Empire by Theodosius' sons.

5th century

410   King Alaric of the Visigoths captures Rome.

455   Capture and sack of Rome by the Vandals.

476   Emperor Romulus Augustus is deposed by Odoacer. End of the Western Empire.

Roman Empire

452   Attila the Hun invades northern Italy.

493   Ostrogoths drive out Odoacer.

6th century

535–553   Emperor Justinian re-conquers the Western Empire from Constantinople.

568   King Albion leads a Lombard invasion.

8th century

752   Pope Gregory invites the Franks to invade under King Pepin.

756   Franks overthrow the Lombards and establish the Papal States (which survive until 1870).

774   Charlemagne (Pepin's son) becomes Emperor.

9th century

800   Charlemagne proclaimed and crowned Emperor by Pope Leo III in Rome.

814   Death of Charlemagne. Resultant anarchy leads to creation of many rival states with fortified walled towns.

831   Moslems invade Sicily and make Palermo their capital.

878   Moslem civilization established in Sicily.

10th century

951   Intervention in Italy by Otto I, King of the Lombards.

Holy Roman Empire

962   Otto I is Crowned Emperor and founds the Holy Roman
Empire. Germanic succession assured until 1806.

11th century

Normans progressively establish themselves in Sicily and the
Southern States of Italy.

12th century

1155   Frederick ('Barbarossa') crowned Holy Roman Emperor.
Struggles between the Pope and Emperor resume. Supporters of
the Emperor are known as the Ghibelines and Papal supporters as
Guelphs.

1167   Creation of association of Guelph cities in Lombardy (the
Lombard League).

1176   Frederick Barbarossa reconciles with Pope Alexander III.

13th century

Struggle continues between Frederick Barbarossa and the Pope.

1220   Frederick II, grandson of Barbarossa, comes to the throne
of Southern Italy. Moslems and Jews granted freedom of religion.
Northern states free themselves from feudal control and set up
family run semi-autonomous governments (the 'Signorias') under
the protection of either the Emperor or the Pope.

1265   Charles of Anjou crowned King of Sicily ousting German
rule.

1282   Increased taxes lead to uprising (the 'Sicilian Vespers') in
which French settlers massacred.

14th century

1302   Angevin dynasty established in Naples.

1303   King Philip of France attacks Pope Boniface VIII.

1309–1377   Rival papacy establishes itself in Avignon in France. Avignon popes include Clement V to Gregory XI, who returns the papacy to Rome.

The Renaissance
15th century

Throughout the 15th and early 16th centuries, the centre and north of the country are transformed by the upsurge of large-scale goods production, greatly improved trade and above all the flowering of art, literature and music. The arts flourish at the courts of the Italian rulers, in particular the families of the Medici in Florence, the Sforza in Milan, the Montefeltro in Urbino, the Este in Ferrara, the Gonzaga in Mantua and the Popes in Rome.

1402   German Emperor's last military intervention defeated by Lombard militia.

1418   The Great Schism of the West (anti-popes in Pisa and Avignon), which started in 1378, is ended by Council of Constance.

1442   King Alfonso V, King of Aragon becomes King of the Two Sicilies.

1453   Fall of Constantinople to the Turks.

1492   Death of Lorenzo de Medici (the 'Magnificent'). Genoan navigator, Christopher Columbus, discovers America.

1494   Giacomo Savonarola preaches against the Pope and the Church in Florence.

1498   Savonarola burned at the stake in Florence for heresy.
16th century

France and Spain engaged in struggle for the supremacy of Europe.

1515–1526   François I, King of France, is forced to give up the Italian heritage.

1527   Emperor Charles V's troops sack Rome.

During the second half the 16th century, the Church of Rome responds to the rise of Protestantism (initiated by Martin Luther in Germany) by instructing the judicial arm of the Church (the Inquisition) to search out heresy. The resulting reign of terror lasts for nearly 100 years.

17th century

Spanish gain domination over the district of Milan, Naples, Sicily and Sardinia which lasts until the early 18th century. The Inquisition continues throughout Europe.

18th century

1700   Death of Emperor Charles II (last of the Hapsburgs).

1713   Victor Amadeus II of Savoy becomes King of Sicily.

1720   Duke of Savoy exchanges Sicily for Sardinia.

1796   Napoleon Bonaparte leads campaign in Lombardy. Declares himself Dictator.

1799   Napoleon declares himself First Consul of Italy. Italy proclaimed a Republic by Napoleon.

19th century

1805   Napoleon transforms Italian Republic into Kingdom with himself as King.

1808   Rome is occupied by French troops.

1809   Papal States are annexed by the French Empire.

1814   Napoleon defeated and exiled. He dies in 1821. End of Napoleonic rule over Europe.

1815   Congress of Vienna. Italy divided up and pre-Napoleonic rulers reinstated.

Risorgimento (Towards Italian Unity)

1830/31   Young Italy founded by Giuseppe Manzini. Growth of anti-Austrian feeling.

1834–1837   Uprisings in Genoa and the kingdom of the Two Sicilies.

1848   First War of Independence against Austria.

1848–1861   Uprisings all over Italy. Victor Emmanuelle II succeeds to the throne of Italy. Cesare Balbo and Camillo Benso di
Cavour found the newspaper 'Il Risorgimento' in Turin to dissemi-
nate nationalist ideas. Garibaldi and his volunteer force, 'the One
Thousand', liberate Sicily and southern Italy from the Bourbons.

1861   Kingdom of Italy proclaimed with Turin as capital and Victor
Emmanuelle II as King.

1866   War of Independence with Prussians. Veneto is annexed.

1870   Italian troops recapture Rome. Unification of Italy is complete. Papal troops resist Italians. Pope Pius IX stripped of his temporal powers.

Rise of Modern Italy

1882   Italy, France and Germany sign the Triple Alliance.

1885   Italy gains a foothold in Eritrea and Somalia.

20th century

1900   King Umberto is assassinated by an anarchist. Accession
of King Victor Emmanuelle III.

1904–1906   Period of rapprochement between Italy, Britain and
France.

1914   Start of World War I. Italy joins the war on side of Britain and
France.
Benito Mussolini starts his newspaper, 'Popolo d'Italia,' supporting
the allied cause.

1918   End of World War I.

1919   Mussolini founds the Italian Fascist Party.

1921   Social uprisings instigated by the Fascist Party.

1922–1926   Mussolini marches on Rome. The king asks him to
form a government. He declares himself Il Duce and becomes
dictator of Italy.

1929   Italy and the Vatican sign the Lateran Treaty declaring
Catholicism the official religion of Italy and recognizing the Vatican

as an independent state. The Pope recognizes the unified
Kingdom of Italy.

1936   Italy occupies Ethiopia. Forms alliance with Adolf Hitler,
fascist dictator of Germany. Rome-Berlin axis formed.

1940/41   Italy joins the war against Britain and France on the side
of Germany.

1943   10 July, Allied armies land in Sicily. 25 July, Mussolini is
overthrown and arrested. 12 Sept., Mussolini set free by Germans.
Italian Socialist Republic set up in Northern Italy.

1944   Mussolini captured trying to flee the country. He is tried and
shot.

1945   25 April, Italy is liberated.
End of World War II in Europe.

1946   May, King Victor Emmanuelle abdicates and is succeeded
by Umberto II. June, constitutional monarchy abolished. Republic
declared after referendum.

1947   Treaty of Paris. France loses colonies and Albania, Istria,
Dalmatia and the Dodocanese.

1948   New Italian constitution comes into effect.

1954   Trieste attached to Italy.

1957   Italy becomes one of 6 founding members of the European
Economic Community (EEC).

1963   Aldo Moro appointed Prime Minister.

1968–1980   Social unrest throughout Italy.

1970   Ultra-right-wing groups active in Italy. Socialist terrorist
group, Red Brigade, founded.

1978   Aldo Moro captured by the Red Brigade and assassinated.
Government appoints Carlo Alberto dalla Chiesa to wipe out terrorist groups. (He is assassinated in Palermo in 1980 while investigat-
ing the Mafia).

1992   Arrest of Socialist Party worker sparks off corruption scandal (Tangentopoli).

1994   Silvio Berlusconi leads a right wing coalition (Freedom Alliance) made up of neo-fascist Alleanza Nationale and the federalist Northern League. 9 months later Berlusconi is forced to resign over corruption charges.

1996   Elections return centre-left coalition (l'Ulivo – Olive Tree) under Romano Prodi. Rifondazione Communista joins the alliance.

1996–present   Centre-left 'l'Ulivo' and centre-right ' Il Polo' (the Freedom Alliance without the Northern League) dominate Italy's political scene.

CULTURAL BRIEFING

Architecture and Design

Greek and Etruscan

8th–5th centuries BC

The Greeks started settling in the southern part of Italy in the 8th century BC and left an extensive architectural heritage of temples, theatres etc. behind. In Magna Graecia, in the south of Italy, the temples of Paestum, Selinus and Agrigento are magnificent examples of vigorous Doric architecture whereas the delicate temple at Segesta perfectly reflects the Ionic style. Well-preserved theatres can still be seen at Syracuse, Segesta and Taormina (although at Taormina the theatre was almost completely re-built by the Romans).

While the Greeks were civilising the southern part of Italy, the Etruscans were occupying the area between the Arno and the Tiber rivers. Etruscan towns were well planned and built on elevated sites surrounded by walls constructed from huge stones.

4th century BC

The war between Sparta and Athens impoverished the Greek world and a decline in architecture and building resulted. The emphasis switched away from full scale building to decorative sculpture and much of the sculpture that adorned the temples of this period can now be seen in the museums of Naples, Paestum, Reggio-Calabria, Taranto and, in Sicily, Palermo and Syracuse.

The Romans

8th century BC–476 AD

Rome was founded in the 8th century BC and from then until the end of the Western Empire in 476 AD, Roman architecture dominated the peninsula. Its effects and influences can be seen in Italian architecture of every period all over Italy to this day. The art of building was highly developed by the Romans and their towns were well planned. Paved streets were edged with footpaths and lined with porticoes to shelter the pedestrians. The houses were built around a central atrium with rooms leading off the central courtyard. Each town was built around a forum, originally a market place, which later became a meeting place and the commercial hub of a town and the location of government offices. Nearby, public baths were available for all the inhabitants and were widely used. They had complex systems of piping hot and cold water through a series of rooms whose floors and pools were covered with elaborate and colourful mosaics. Triumphal arches were built at the entrances of towns to commemorate the victory or triumph of a general or emperor and temples were constructed for the worship of the many gods and goddesses that made up Roman religion. The Roman style had evolved from the Greek style with columns and colonnades, although Roman design was heavier and more solid in appearance than the Greek. The Romans built amphitheatres and this typically Roman structure was several stories high, encircling an oval arena with seating for the spectators. The Roman city of Pompeii was frozen in time when the nearby volcano Mt. Vesuvius erupted and cast it in molten lava,

preserving perfect examples of Roman architecture. Pompeii's
thermal baths and amphitheatre are amongst the earliest
examples of their kind and it is also possible to see an early
basilica, homes of the rich and well-to-do Romans and many simpler dwellings. The town provides a very good idea of how the
Romans lived and what their domestic architecture looked like.
Elsewhere, Ostia Antica has examples of well preserved 'insulae',
a kind of ancient multi-storey apartment block much like the apartment buildings of today, and Rome itself is full of archaeological
remains. The Coliseum is the largest and most famous example of
a Roman amphitheatre ever built and the Baths of Caracalla are
probably the most elaborate and complex example of Roman
Baths *(for more details see Rome, page 74).*

Byzantine and Early Christian

5th–11th centuries

The earliest examples of Christian architecture are the secret
burial places of the early Christians, the Catacombs. The network
of galleries were carved out of the soft rock near Rome and were
used by groups of persecuted Christians as places of worship as
well as burial grounds. When the Emperor Constantine legalized
Christianity in 313 AD churches began to spring up, often in
adapted existing Roman structures. Early Christian basilicas
followed the Roman style of building in shape and design. The first
Christian church of this period was the original basilica of
St. Peter's in Rome and it was built in the basic Roman Basilican
style which continued to be used for centuries all over Italy. The art
and architecture of Byzantium, best known for the richness of its
mosaic decoration, evolved from this early Christian style and
flourished in Italy between the 8th and 11th centuries after
Constantine had moved the seat of the Roman Empire to
Constantinople. The capital of Italian Byzantine art was Ravenna,

although Rome, Sicily, parts of Lombardy and Venice carried on
the tradition until well into the 13th century. The Basilica of St. Mark
in Venice was modelled on the Church of the Holy Apostles – now
destroyed – in Constantinople, complete with bulbous domes and
Greek-cross floor plan.

Romanesque

11th–12th centuries

Italian Romanesque, with its generous rounded arches and heavy
walls, had evolved directly out of the Roman basilica with influences from the orient and, later on in the 12th century, from the
Norman and Provincial architectural traditions. Italian
Romanesque can be divided into regional styles. The Lombardy
churches, best illustrated by the Duomo at Modena, were typically
built with carved façades decorated with contrasting bands of
marble or other stone. The 'campanile' (bell towers) were usually
detached from the main body of the church. The Pisan style was
similar to the Lombardy style but with a greater Byzantine influence. The churches and other religious buildings had tiers of
arcades and many small columns with blind archways and
decorative marble inlay all over the façade. The Duomo,
Baptistry and the famous 'leaning' tower best illustrate this style.
The Florentine Romanesque remained highly individual and
within the confines of the city. The simple lines of the façades
were decorated with grey-green interspersed with white marbles.
In Latium and Campania, the churches were decorated by the
Consati – a guild of mosaic and marble workers who specialized
in decorating floors, Episcopal thrones and pulpits, with multi-
coloured marble fragments. In the south and in Sicily, the
Romanesque style combined with Moorish, Byzantine and
Norman tendencies to produce a highly decorative and
individual style.

Gothic

13th–14th centuries

Gothic architecture originated in France and it was the Cistercians who did most to spread the new style throughout Italy. They built a series of monasteries starting with the Abbey of Fossanova. They were swiftly copied, first by the Franciscans with the Basilica of San Francesco in Assisi and then by the Dominicans with the Church of Santa Maria Novella in Florence. The Gothic style with its flying buttresses and tall slender archways that dominated church building throughout northern Europe well into the 14th century was not so popular in Italy. However there are some magnificent examples of Italian Gothic – the Cathedrals of Milan and Sienna, the Basilica of San Pietronio in Bologna and the Church of the Frari in Venice. The Gothic style was widely used in public buildings and palaces and many of the more prosperous towns enriched their town centres with grand gothic municipal palaces. In Venice, Gothic palaces along the Grand Canal alternate with their Romanesque, Renaissance, Classical and Baroque neighbours while the Palazzo Ducale in Venice and the Palazzo Pubblico in Sienna are both fine examples of public buildings in the Gothic style.

The Holy Roman Emperor, Frederick II, built Castel del Monte near Bari in Apulia combining an octagonal plan taken from Roman buildings with elements of French Gothic.

Renaissance

Quattrocento

(15th century)

The Renaissance was the richest period in Italian cultural history in which all the arts flourished. Innovation was an important aspect of this period and a renewed interest in the classical works was combined with a rejection of dogmatic religious authority. Florence was at the cultural and artistic heart of the Renaissance and the ruling family, the Medicis, were the biggest patrons that century, encouraging and commissioning artists from every discipline. Among the many architects, two men, Filippo Bruneleschi and Leon Battista Alberti stand out. Bruneleschi started life as a goldsmith and sculptor but turned his hand to architecture and built the first Renaissance building in Florence, the Spedale degli Innocenti. His later design for the first major dome of the Duomo still baffles architects. Alberti was a poet and humanist and was the first Italian architect to incorporate town planning into his architectural ideas. Among his most famous designs are the Tempio Malatestiano in Rimini, the churches of Sant' Andrea in Mantua and the Palazzo Rucella in Florence. He is also responsible for the façade of Santa Maria Novella in Florence.

15th–16th centuries

The High Renaissance is dominated by three of the greatest men of Italian arts, Leonardo da Vinci, Michelangelo, and Raphael. Leonardo was more an inventor, weapons designer, musician, engineer, scientist and artist than an architect, but nevertheless he exerted a powerful influence on the design and architecture of the day. Michelangelo, more painter and sculptor than architect, designed the Dome of St. Peter's in Rome. Among other notable architects working at this time, Donato Bramante invented the 'rhythmic bay' – a façade comprised of windows, niches and pilasters. He worked in Milan and Urbino before working on the original Greek-Cross plan for St. Peter's in Rome. Raphael succeeded him as the architect of St Peter's in Rome and in turn was succeeded by Antonio Sangallo. Bramante went on to design the Palazzo Farnese (later the French Embassy) in Rome. Andrea Palladio is best known for his 'Ville Venete' – palatial villas in the Venetian plain. Among his religious works are the Rotunda in Verona and the Chiesa del Redentore in Venice. His own classical style was inspired by Roman buildings and his 'Four Books on Architecture' helped to rekindle interest in the Classical style.

Mannerism

16th–17th centuries

The art and architecture of Mannerism used the basic principles of the Renaissance while altering them in an extreme or 'mannered' way. Mannerism is also known as the art of the counter-reformation and the austere lines and formality reflect prevailing religious feeling. The Mannerist style can also be seen in the juxtaposition of nature and artificiality in the many gardens and palace grounds designed during this period. The church of Gesù in Rome, an austere building created by the architect Giacomo Barozzi da Vignola, and the Palazzo del Te in Mantua, built by Giuliano Romano, are perhaps the most important examples of Italian Mannerist churches.

Baroque

17th–18th centuries

The Baroque sprang up in reaction to the austerity of the Mannerist style. Unlike the cold grandeur of the Mannerist churches and palaces, the Baroque buildings were elaborate, ornate and theatrical, often decorated in fantastical styles. The elaborate façade of St. Peter's in Rome was designed by Carlo Maderno, one of Italy's most influential Baroque architects. The influence of Lorenzo Bernini, who built the colonnades of St. Peter's Square, virtually transformed Rome into the Baroque city we see today. Francesco Borromini revolutionized accepted architectural practise by using space and light to create effects and illusions. Further south, in Apulia, the city of Lessee remains one of the most complete and perfect examples of the Spanish-influenced High Baroque style, and Noto in Sicily and much of Naples also reflect this style.

Neo-Classical

Late 18th–19th centuries

Throughout this period, the pure and simple lines of the classical style once again became the fashion all over Europe. Of the Italian Neo-classical architects perhaps the most outstanding was Alessandro Antonelli, who adopted the Neo-classical style for the unusual buildings he created in Milan and his native town, Novara.

20th century

Early in the 20th century, an architect of the futurist movement, Antonio Sant'Elia, led the way in the development of modern Italian architecture with his unrealized plans for a high-tech high rise Città Nuova.

Fascist Style

In the 1920s and 1930s, Marcello Piacentini became the leading exponent of the heavy grandiose style of building and often mis-guided town planning favoured by Mussolini. Among other things, he built the Stadio dei Marmi at Rome's Stadio Olimpico and the Esposizione Universale di Roma, a satellite city that has now become a Roman suburb.

Post-War Years

Italy has produced some very fine post-war architects. Among them, Pier-Luigi Nervi and Gio Ponti are perhaps the best known. They both pioneered the use of reinforced concrete and plastics and Ponti's Pirelli Tower near the main railway station in Milan is regarded as one of Europe's finest skyscrapers. Nervi built the futuristic soccer stadium in Florence and an audience hall for Pope Paul VI in the Vatican.

Painting and Sculpture

Etruscan and Roman

8th century BC–4th century AD

Most of what we know of Etruscan painting comes from the tombs at Tarquinia. Happy, lively scenes painted in strong colours represent the Etruscan view that death was a joyous passing from one world to the next. Later on this mood was tempered by the prevailing influence of Greek culture. There is a great deal of Etruscan sculpture, most of it funerary, and the most famous pieces – the Sarcophagus of the Married Couple, and the Apollo of Veii, a terracotta statue from the temple of Veii (both 6th century BC) – are in the Museum of Villa Giulia in Rome. The bronze statue, the Capitoline Wolf, became the symbol of Rome in 296 BC (Romulus and Remus, the suckling twins beneath the wolf, were added in the Renaissance).

The frescoes of Pompeii and Herculaneum are among the only surviving examples of Roman painting left today, and most of those have been removed to the Museo Nazionale in Naples. The 'Odyssey Landscapes', frescoes dating from the 1st century BC, were taken from a Roman nobleman's house on the Esquiline Hill in Rome and are now in the Vatican Library. The Romans based much of their artistic style on the Greeks who had preceded them. Their landscapes and portraits show strong Greek influence, although at the same time Roman sculptors were developing their own realistic style of portrait sculpture, many examples of which can be seen in the Musei Capitolini and the Vatican Museum. Relief sculpture was also very important to the Romans and carved historic military campaigns and victories were depicted on the walls of buildings.

Early Christian and Byzantine

4th–10th centuries

The early Christians decorated the walls of their catacombs with painted frescoes and although the subject matter was more concerned with spiritual values than physical beauty, the style the artists used was much the same as that of their pagan Roman contemporaries. After Constantine recognized and legalized the Christian religion, the Christian artists started to use Byzantine techniques. The early churches of that period were decorated with elaborate mosaics and tesserae of reflective glass fragments designed to catch the light and emphasise the subject matter. Santa Constanza in Rome (mid-4th century) is a good example of this blend of Byzantine and Christian styles. Although the Early Christians rejected free standing statues as being too reminiscent of pagan gods, they did use the Roman technique of relief sculpture, but mainly to adorn their sarcophagi. The Eastern Roman Empire developed into the Byzantine Empire and the transition resulted in the development of mosaic technique and style. The Mosaics at Ravenna which date from 5th and 6th centuries show abstract and symbolic subject matter while those in the Basilica at Ravenna show the Emperor Justinian and his wife illustrated in the earlier style. Venice has fine examples of the later mosaics, especially in the Basilica of San Marco and the Basilica of Santa Maria Assunta on the island of Torcello, and in Rome there are several churches decorated during this period.

The Middle Ages

Romanesque

11th–12th centuries

The religious art of the Romanesque period in Italy revived the art of carved statuary that had almost been lost during the previous three centuries. Churches were decorated with figurative stone-carved sculptures of saints and religious figures. Mosaic and tesserae work was still used and the Cosmati – a guild of craftsmen from Rome – used multi-coloured marbles as well as gilded mosaics to adorn the churches in Latium and Campania.

In southern Italy and Sicily, the combined styles of the Lombards, the Normans, the Moors and Byzantium resulted in church decoration that, although essentially religious in nature, was also highly decorative.

Gothic

13th and 14th centuries.

The painted relief crucifixes that appeared in the 12th century were the first examples of Italian painting and over the next hundred years the rigid Byzantine style began to relax. The Pisano family in Pisa provided Italy with two of its most famous gothic sculptors, Giovanni with his vigorous new realism and Nicola with his continued use of classical techniques. Their works are to be found in the Cathedral and Baptistery in Pisa. The Siennese school produced artists like Duccio di Buoninsegna and Simone Martini, both of whose work still showed a strong Byzantine influence. In the early 13th century, the Florentine painter Cimabue decorated the Upper Basilica of San Francesco in Assisi with frescoes that illustrated a new naturalism and sense of pathos in the facial expressions of his subjects. Cimabue greatly influenced Giotto, who developed the techniques even further and revolutionized Italian painting with his passionate approach and the depth of feeling in his painting. Giotto was a humanist who rejected many of the traditional attitudes of the medieval world, as illustrated by his idiosyncratic depiction of familiar scenes from the Bible stories. His work can be seen primarily in and around Florence and in the Cappella di Scrivegni in Padova. By the14th century, communications in Europe had greatly improved and the influence of French and Spanish work began to be felt. This resulted in the development of the so-called International Gothic, a style that refined and exaggerated the deceptive elements of gothic painting while approaching the subject matter in a more humanistic manner. The leading proponents of this style included Gentile da Fabriano who was working in the northern part of Italy, the Veronese painter Pisanello, the Florentine artists Andrea Orcagna and Andrea di Firenze.

Renaissance

15th century

(Quattrocento)   Donatello was the first sculptor to create a bronze free-standing figure since ancient times and his statue of David (now in Florence's Museo Bargello) shows the anatomical realism that was such an important part of Renaissance sculpture. His contemporary, Luca della Robbia, created a new art form with his glazed coloured terracotta representations of religious subjects. Lorenzo Ghiberti covered the huge doors of the Baptistery (the 'Gates of Paradise') in Florence with strips of bronze relief depicting stories form the Bible. Florence was at the heart of the Renaissance with the ruling family, the Medicis, attracting artists from all over Italy. The new era of painting was one of innovation and technical skill, and of these artists Massaccio was one of the first painters to place emphasis on an illusion of perspective. Paolo Uccello used a foreshortening technique to bring his battle scenes alive and even Fra Angelico, who remained very faithful to the gothic ideals of painting, was attracted to the new techniques. Fra Filippo Lippi painted with delicacy and piety and also taught one of the great masters of the Quattrocento, Sandro Botticelli. One of the principal recipients of Medici patronage, Botticelli drew for inspiration on pagan allegories as well as religious subjects and his 'Birth of Venus' and 'Spring' are world famous examples of renaissance Florentine painting. Piero della Francesca was trained in Florence under the painter Domenico Veneziano, but spent most of his life working in and around Arezzo and Urbino. Among his many masterpieces is the magnificent series of frescoes in the church of San Francesco in Arezzo. At the Gonzaga court of Mantua, Andrea Mantegna was fascinated by architecture and anatomy while

Venice produced the Bellini family, Jacopo and his two sons, Gentile and Giovanni (who was also the brother-in-law of Mantegna). All three painted with sensitivity and filled the churches and palaces of Venice with altar pieces, luminous landscapes and portraits. Venice was also home to Giorgione and Perugino (whose student was Raphael).

16th century

(Cinquecento)   At the beginning of the 16th century, the centre of the renaissance shifted away from Florence to Rome. A series of Popes – Alexander VI, Julius II, Leo X and Clement VII – took the lead of the Florentine Medicis and patronized the greatest artists of the day to enrich the churches and palaces of Rome and the Vatican. The three main figures of the High Renaissance were Leonardo da Vinci, Michelangelo and Raphael. Michelangelo was a painter and sculptor of great power. His sculptures include the 'Pietà' in St. Peters, the gigantic figure of David in Florence (now in the Galleria dell'Accademia) and the 'Moses' in the Roman church, San Pietro in Vincoli. Having come to Rome to design the tomb of Pope Julius II he was commissioned to paint the ceiling of the Sistine chapel, a task that took him many years. In his powerful figures can be seen the origins of Roman Mannerism. After finishing the ceiling Michelangelo did not paint again until, twenty three years later, he was recalled to the Sistine Chapel to paint The Last Judgement behind the high altar. He died in Florence after sculpting the tombs of the Medicis. Leonardo Da Vinci's diverse talents gave rise to the expression 'Renaissance Man' referring to the ability of one artist to excel in many disciplines. He painted (his most famous work being 'The Last Supper' in the Vinciano Refectory next to Milan's Chiesa di Santa Maria delle Grazie), he sculpted, he studied human anatomy in order to improve human proportional definition, he perfected the aerial perspective, and he revolutionized painting in Europe with his 'sfumato' technique (literally 'mist') which allowed him to change from colour to colour with great delicacy and subtlety. After having worked in Milan and Florence, Leonardo went to France at the invitation of the King, François I. Raphael was known as the master of Classicism and his works are to be found in museums all over the world. He painted portraits and is famous for his tenderly portrayed Madonnas, as well as for decorating rooms in the Vatican with magnificent frescoes (Stanze di Rafaello). Other important artists of the High Renaissance include Tintoretto, Andrea del Sarto, Correggio, Titian (a disciple of Giovanni Bellini who painted portraits, as well as mythological and religious subjects) and Paolo Veronese, whose mural decorations adorn many of the Palladian 'Villas' of the Veneto and who was known for his crowds of people in classical architectural settings.

Mannerism

16th–17th centuries

Charles V sacked Rome in 1527 and ushered in the start of a new artistic era. Mannerism was also known as the art of the Counter Reformation. In painting this was expressed through the portrayal of idealized beauty and style rather than the naturalism of the Renaissance. The elongated figures in Mannerist paintings are bathed in violent light and give an impression of anxiety and tension that reflected the social conditions of the day. Important Mannerist painters include Jacopo Pontormo, Rosso Fiorentino (both followers of Andrea del Sarto), Bronzino and Giorgio Vasari (also an art historian of note), Benvenuto Cellini and Giovanni di Bologna (also remembered for his superb sculpture).

Baroque

17th–18th centuries

The most famous of Rome's Baroque painters was Michelangelo da Caravaggio. He painted with strength and vigour and his outspoken attitudes towards beauty and ugliness revolutionized centuries of Italian idealism and made him one of the most influential painters of the 17th century. Other notable Baroque artists included Guido Reni, Luca Giordano (in Florence) and Annibale Carracci, who was a member of the Bolognese group of artists who founded the Academy of the Eclectic (Incamminati). Venetian Baroque painting is remembered for its serenity and the canvasses of both Canaletto and Guardi give a vivid and accurate portrayal of Venetian life in the 18th century. Giambattista Tiepolo was the last of the great Italian decorative painters. Painting in Venice, he created many memorable frescoes using vivid colours. Baroque art is most famous for sculpture and Rome was transformed by the works of the sculptors working there, in particular Bernini and Borromini. Bernini produced many famous works of sculpture and Roman fountains, among them the Fontana di Quattro Fiumi (the Fountain of the Four Rivers) which is in the centre of the Piazza Navona. The carved figures on the fountain appear to recoil in horror at the sight of a façade of the Chiesa di Sant'Agnese in Agonia by his rival, Borromini. Nicola Salvi, another important Baroque sculptor, was responsible for the Fontana di Trevi, which was supplied with water by one of Rome's oldest aqueducts.

Neo-Classicism
18th–19th centuries

Antonio Canova was the best known proponent of Neo-Classical sculpture and his statue of Pauline Borghese which is in the Museo Borghese in Rome displays a rather cold simplicity and purity of line reminiscent of works of antiquity that inspired this movement in Italian art.

In painting, the Macciolo group started a revolt in 1885 against academism that lasted for nearly 20 years and gave rise to the paintings of Giovanni Fattori, Sylvestro Lega and Telemaco

Signorini (who travelled widely and is known for his paintings of Edinburgh and London). They were considered to be the precursors of Impressionism and three painters of this period actually went to Paris to study with the Impressionists – de Nittis, Boldoni and Zandomenighi. At the end of the 19th century, Segantini led the transition into the 20th century with his Divisionist school of painting.

20th century

Futurism   This avant garde movement was founded by the theorist and poet, Marinetti, who, together with the painters Boccioni, Balla, Severini and Carrà (who later joined the Surrealists), proclaimed their belief in the mechanical age of speed, and portrayed the modern world by means of fragmented forms not unlike cubism. The movement's preoccupation with machinery acted as a propaganda tool for the First World War. Giorgio Chirico invented metaphysical painting but perhaps the most notable of Italian artists in the years leading up to World War I was Amadeo Modigliani. He went to live in Paris and his distinctive paintings and portraits of elongated women with oval faces were born out of a dissolute life of drugs and alcohol that led to his death at the age of 36.

Post-War Years

Notable sculptors include Arturo Martini, whose work paved the way for a return to archaic art, and his follower, Marino Marini, whose style is similar but much less angular and passionate. Giacomo Manzù has also made an impact.

Italy has a thriving and vibrant contemporary art scene that is centred around Rome and Milan.

Literature

Ancient Rome

3rd–1st centuries BC

The written word from Ancient Rome comes down to us in the form of popular songs, religious ceremonies and some official documents.

As the Latin language developed and contacts with Greek scholars grew, the classic period of Latin literature appeared. Plautus used classical Greek themes to create his own plays.

The politically minded Cicero wrote 'Brutus' as Rome declined into civil war and dictatorial government, while Catullus concentrated on passionate love poetry. Julius Caesar recorded his military campaigns in Gaul and the disintegration of the Roman Empire. Among the many literary figures in the reign of Augustus, Virgil wrote the epic poem 'The Aeneid' and Ovid caused controversy with his love poems 'Ars Amatoria' and 'Amores'. Livy was a historian of Rome from its founding to his own time and Horace wrote verses, among them 'Odes, Epistles, Epodes and Satires'.

1st century BC–1st century AD

During the early Christian era, the Spanish philosopher Seneca wrote reflective and philosophical prose. Our knowledge of the eruption of Vesuvius and the destruction of Pompeii comes from Pliny the Younger's first hand descriptions of the disaster. Petronius recorded the decadence of Nero's reign in his 'Satyricon' (the film director Fellini based his film on the only remaining fragment of this work to survive). Nero's downfall was chronicled in the 'Histories' of Tacitus and the political intrigues of his court are described in his 'Annales'. As his Empire crumbled, the philosopher king, Marcus Aurelius, recorded his personal thoughts in 'Meditations'.

Middle Ages

13th century

In the years between the end of the Roman Empire and the begin-ning of the 13th century the written literary tradition only survived because of the work of a few religious scholars and intellectuals. They debated points of theology, recorded history, and interpreted and translated classical Greek and Roman literature. However, their language was Latin, and among the first examples of writing in the Italian language are the 'Canticles of the Creatures', written by St. Francis of Assisi in the early 13th century. Also at the start of the 13th century, at the court of King Frederick II, the Sicilian School emerged with a language of love that grew out of the traditional ballads from Provence. The most famous school of poetry was the 'Stile Nuovo' which gave us Dante Alighieri. The followers of this school of poetry used a lyrical style to describe spiritual love in verse and Dante used the new technique to write his masterpiece 'Divina Commedia'. This allegory in three parts, 'Inferno', 'Purgatorio', and 'Paradiso', not only describes the search for God but also gives us a vivid picture of the Christianized western world at that time. Dante's Latin work, De Monarchia, on the other hand, reflects his vision of an imperial world, with Popes and Emperors sharing the power.

14th century

Francesco Petrarca (Petrarch) was the son of a lawyer who had been exiled from Florence and after he had earned an international reputation for his classical scholasticism, he was crowned poet laureate in Rome in 1341. His sonnets, 'Il Canzoniere,' together with his epic poem 'Africa' use a vigorous form of lyricism that has continued to influence Italian poets to this day. Giovanni Boccaccio's 'Decameron' was a collection of 100 short stories following 10 young Florentines as they flee from their plague-ridden city. It is said that Boccaccio influenced the

English writer Chaucer and inspired him to write 'The Canterbury Tales'.

Renaissance

15th century

The humanism of the 15th century paid great attention to the translation and reinterpretation of the Greek and Roman classics and also invented a form of scholarly poetry that reflected the soul's aspiration towards an ideal. Aldo Manuzio founded a Greek Academy that published vast numbers of Greek Classics from his Aldine Press. Manuzio introduced italic script and the Octavo, a size of paper half as big as the Quarto and much more manageable and suitable for printed books.

16th century

During the 16th century, writers and poets at the royal courts strove to perfect the written language, and as a result Italian entered a period of great refinement and elegance. One of the most famous statesmen, political theorists and playwrights of the era was Machiavelli, whose enduring political treatise, 'Il Principe' (the Prince) explored the processes which rule human society and examined the political and moral consequences of human relationships. Two of his contemporaries, Ludovico Ariosto and Torquato Tasso, were both luminaries of the Renaissance. Ariosto's 'Orlando Furioso', a complex tale of chivalry, and Tasso's narrative poems, 'Gerusalemme Liberata,' provided the courts where they worked with an element of intellectual brilliance.

Counter-Reformation & Baroque

17th–18th centuries

Galileo was a scientist who challenged the accepted thinking on all the laws governing the physical world and whose writings were vigorously opposed by a Catholic Church in the throes of trying to resist the onslaught of the Protestant reformation. During this period, the Inquisition prevented much growth and development of original thought and, apart from Galileo, Italian literature went into decline.

Age of Enlightenment & Romanticism

18th century

The early part of the 18th century saw the arrival of a literary academy, Arcadia, which advocated 'good taste', an ideal drawn from the purity and rustic simplicity of classical poetry, against the 'bad taste' of the Baroque period. Leading figures of this movement were the philosopher, Giambattista Vico, and the dramatist Metastasio. The 18th century was dominated, however, by the dramatist Carlo Goldoni. He brought Italian drama to the forefront of European theatre with his witty intellectual plays written round a set of stock characters in the style of the Commedia del'Arte, a style of dramatic writing popular in Venice at the time.

19th century

Poetry was Romanticism's main contribution to Italian literature and Giacomo Leopardi was one of its principal proponents. His 'Canti' was a collection of erudite and melancholic poems reflecting the prevailing dichotomy between the natural or 'happy' state and the contrasting state of 'Reason' which brought unhappiness. Other poets included Gabriele d'Annunzio who expressed his sensual approach to love in a refined style, and Giovanni Pascoli whose poetry was filled with nostalgia for an age of innocence. Later in the century, the Milanese writer, Alessandro Manzoni, wrote 'I Promessi Sposi' (The Betrothed), an epic historical work that was perhaps the most important Italian novel of the 19th century. Giovanni Vega's 'I Malavoglia' was the first 'realist' novel and it marked the transition into the 20th century. In Sicily, Giuseppe di Lampedusa wrote 'Il Gattopardo' (The Leopard), a novel that movingly tells the story of a family at the time of reunification and the decline of the feudal system in Sicily. The book, which is the only work by Lampedusa to be remembered, was made into a film by Luchino Visconti.

20th century

Early in the 20th century, a number of political, moral, cultural and literary periodicals appeared and attracted contributions from all the major writers of the day including Giuseppe Prezzollini and Giovanni Papini. The world of Italian letters followed the same line as other European literary schools and expressed the themes of discovery, inspired by the rise of psychoanalysis that was emanating from writers like Kafka, Proust and Joyce. Perhaps the best known dramatist of the first half of the 20th century was the Sicilian, Luigi Pirandello. He wrote such classics as 'Sei Personaggi in Cerca d'Autore' (Six Characters in Search of an Author), and the way in which his works changed the concept of what theatre could be has influenced generations of modern playwrights and earned him a Nobel Prize in 1934. Other key poets included Giuseppe Ungaretti and Eugenio Montale. Salvatore Quasimodo, who was the leader of the Hermetic Movement, produced many well-received translations of Greek and Roman classical literature and Shakespeare.

The rise of neo-realism in literature produced works that were full of the misery of life for the working classes, peasants and street children, themes that lent themselves readily to the new art form of the cinema.

Italy has produced a rich legacy of fiction, with classic novels being written and published not only in Italian but in most of the major languages of the world. Leading writers of contemporary Italian fiction include Cesare Pavese who wrote 'La Luna e il Falo' (The Moon and the Bonfire) and Carlo Levi, the Turin doctor exiled to southern Italy under the fascists, who wrote 'Cristo si è Fermato a Eboli' (Christ Stopped at Eboli). Primo Levi, another Jew who ended up in Auschwitz, wrote Se Quest'è un Uomo (If This is a Man), an account of his survival, and La Tregua (The Truce) which recounts his long journey home after the war. After the war, Natalia Ginzburg wrote largely autobiographical works while the works of Italo Calvino dwell on a fantastical view of human behaviour, most notably in his novel 'I Nostri Antenati' (Our Ancestors). Alberto Moravia's most famous work, 'La Romana' (The Roman Woman), describes the decline of a Roman family. The novels of Rome's Else Morante display a subtle psychological approach to characterisation, and in her novel 'Menzoga e Sortilegio' she describes the slow decay of a noble family in southern Italy. Outside Italy, perhaps the best known of the country's authors is the popular Umberto Eco, whose first book 'Il Nome della Rosa' (The Name of the Rose) shot him into the international limelight and was made into a successful film.

Music

10th century

A Benedictine monk, Guido Monaco of Arezzo, invented the musical scale.

16th century

Polyphony had its golden age during the 16th century and Giovanni Pierluigi di Palestrina was one of its leading composers. In Venice, Andrea Gabrielli and his nephew Giovanni were both organists at the Basilica of San Marco and were masters of sacred and secular polyphonic music. As early as the turn of the 16th century, music saw one of its greatest revolutions, the first beginnings of opera. Claudio Monteverdi more or less invented the operatic form creating compositions that combined words and music in the telling of a story. Monteverdi's influence on music has been immeasurable and the form of modern opera was founded on his original principles.

Baroque

17th century

The individual character of Italian music, in both the schools of instrumental and operatic composition, emerged strongly from the 16th century onwards. The first musical scores to be printed on a movable type press came out of Venice during the 16th century and the works of the great Italian Baroque composers went on to be published here, while in Cremona, the Stradivarius family and others were producing fine stringed instruments. Among the major composers of the Baroque period are Frescobaldi, who wrote mostly for the organ, and Corelli, whose instrumental compositions included many works for the violin. The new forms of musical instruments meant a new style of composition and the Venetian school produced composers like Vivaldi, best remembered today for his 'Four Seasons', whose musical influence extended far beyond his native land. Bach was one of many composers to be influenced by his work. Domenico Scarlatti wrote extensively for the harpsichord and Giovanni Battista Sammartini produced some early experimental versions of the modern symphonic form.

18th century

Most of the important Italian composers of the 18th century worked abroad at the courts of the European rulers. Antonio Salieri was a key figure in European music. A Venetian, he taught some of the most famous names in European music including Beethoven, Schubert and Liszt. He was obsessed with Mozart and, while mentally unstable at the end of his life, blamed himself for Mozart's untimely death. Chamber music started to appear in modern form with the works of, among others, Luigi Boccherini. The end of the 18th century saw a Romantic movement sweep Italy and the work of Niccolo Paganini exemplifies the new style. A virtuoso violinist himself, he wrote impossibly difficult romantic works for the violin including many concerti and the famous 24 Cappricci.

19th century

The 19th century was the golden age of Italian opera. By the end of the 17th century, Scarlatti had produced a quantity of Neapolitan operas. In the 18th century, Pergolese, Cimarosa and Paisiello were established as the masters of the Opera Buffa (light or comic opera). But with the turn of the 19th century, Rossini heralded in a new period with operas like William Tell, the Barber of Seville, the Thieving Magpie and the Italian Girl in Algiers, which combined the classical and romantic styles. Bellini wrote melodic works like Norma and La Somnambula while Donizetti wrote melodramas like Lucia di Lammermoor as well as comic operas like L'Elisir d'Amore and Don Pasquale. Probably the best known operatic composer of the 19th century was Giuseppe Verdi. His long list of romantic dramas includes Nabucco, Rigoletto, Il Trovatore and Aida (which was written for the opening of the new Cairo Opera House in 1871). Puccini, who straddled the 19th and 20th centuries, brought the era of romantic Italian opera to a climax with Madame Butterfly, Tosca, La Boheme and others.

20th century

The early part of the 20th century produced a new generation of instrumental composers. Ottorino Respighi composed symphonic poems (the Fountains of Rome, etc) and early experimental composers included Petrassi. One of the first Italian composers to use the 12-tone scale was Dallapiccola, and Luigi Nono's sensitive and passionate music used serial music to express a political message of liberation. After World War II, opera continued to flourish both in performance and with new compositions. Among the most influential composers was Gian Carlo Menotti, who not only wrote his own operas, but also started the now famous annual musical festival at Spoleto. Popular music includes a continuing affection for traditional folk songs which have been sung all over Italy for centuries, the most famous of which being the Canzone Napolitana.

Cinema
1904–1930

The Italian film industry was born in Turin in 1904 and flourished in the early days of silent movies, with more than 50 production companies in operation by 1914. By 1930, however, it was teetering on the edge of bankruptcy and the Mussolini government took over the industry. In 1935, the government set up Cinecittà – Italy's version of Hollywood – and installed the latest equipment into the huge complex of production and sound stages in Rome. Most of the film production in Italy at that time took place at Cinecittà, with more than 85 movies produced in 1940 alone.

Neo-Realism

From 1946 until the early 1950s, the Italian filmmakers concentrated on themes dealing with the war and its aftermath. Roberto Rossellini made two films denouncing fascism and Nazi oppression – 'Roma Città Aperto' (Rome Open City) starring Anna Magnani and 'Germania Anno Zero' (Germany Year Zero). Vittorio de Sica made ten films between 1939 and 1950, among them 'Sciusia' and the 'Ladri di Biciclette' (Bicycle Thieves) which portrayed the misery of unemployment in the post-war years. De Santi's films dealing with the revolutionary ambitions of the working class in Bitter Rice and Bloody Easter brought the period of neo-realism to an end.

1950s

In the early 1950s, Cinecittà began to be used as one of the world's major production studios and, after an American team arrived to make 'Quo Vadis?' in 1950, other American companies started to come to Italy to make films.

1960s

In the early 1960s, location shooting had reduced the importance of Cinecittà as studios, but it was also the start of the golden age of Italian cinema.

Michelangelo Antonioni directed his first film in 1960 and many of his subsequent films explored existential themes. His career reached its height in 1967 with 'Blow-up'.

Pier Paolo Pasolini's early films, such as 'Accetone' (1961) and 'Teporema' (1968), were preoccupied with the social conditions of the working classes. Later works like 'Decameron', 'I Raconti Canterbury' and 'Il Fiore delle Mille e Una Notte' dealt more with themes of human decay and death.

Luchino Visconti's first film was 'Ossessione' (based on James Cain's 'The Postman Always Rings Twice'), but of his many films, perhaps the most famous is his adaptation of Giuseppe di Lampedusa's novel 'Il Gattopardo' (The Leopard). Visconti went on making films right up until his death in 1976.

Federico Fellini was perhaps the most fantastical of the Italian directors. He made a series of disturbing films including 'La Dolce Vita', 'Satyricon', 'Roma' and 'Amacord'. His wife, Giuletta Masina, starred in most of his films.

1970s

Lina Wertmüller's best known work 'Travolta da un Insolito Destino nell'Azzuro Mare di Agosto' (Swept Away) incurred the wrath of feminists the world over. Meanwhile, Bernardo Bertolucci had his first international hit with the controversial erotic film 'Last Tango in Paris'.

1980s–present

Bertolucci went on making international hit films like 'The Last Emperor' and 'The Sheltering Sky'. Franco Zeffirelli has made many films since 1980, among them 'Othello', 'Young Toscanini' and 'Hamlet'.

The film industry in Italy has been under threat from television and international competition, but Italy has produced some remarkable films in recent years. Giuseppe Tornatore's film 'Cinema Paradiso' won him international acclaim and Nanni

Moretti's autobiographical three-part film won the prize for Best Director at the 1994 Cannes Film Festival.

In 1994, French/Italian co-production 'Il Postino' was nominated in various categories by the American Academy and took the 'Oscars' by storm, winning in the best original dramatic score category. Roberto Benigni's 'La Vita è Bella' (Life is Beautiful) won 3 'Oscars' in 1999 – best actor, best foreign-language film and best film music.

In 1996 there were 4,004 cinema screens (1,200 full-time) and 96,512,000 admissions.

MAJOR CITIES

(The international code for telephoning or faxing Italy is the code required to dial out of your own country followed by 39).

ROME (ROMA):

National capital city (1996 population, 2,645,000), capital of Latium and Rome Province in central Italy.

According to legend, Rome was founded in 753 BC by the twin descendants of Aeneas the Trojan, Romulus and Remus. The Trojans ruled Rome with the Sabines until the arrival of the Etruscans in 8th century BC.

The first Republic of Rome was declared in 509 BC and with it the start of the greatest period of Roman expansion. After the assassination of Julius Caesar in 44 BC, Augustus was declared Emperor and God. He strengthened Roman government and restored peace to the entire Roman basin. The spread of Christianity in the 1st and 2nd centuries AD was in defiance of Roman law, but the conversion of the Emperor Constantine in 314 gave Christians the freedom to practise their religion. Rome has always claimed supremacy in the Christian church and through 19 centuries the Popes, who were the original bishops of Rome, have influenced religious and political thinking far beyond the Vatican City (a sovereign state within Rome).

Rome has been the capital of Italy since 1870 when it was a city of 200,000 inhabitants. Today the population numbers close to 3m. Rome is also the capital of Latium, a region of central Italy, and of Rome province. Built on seven hills, the city straddles the banks of the River Tiber. Called the Eternal City, Rome is one of the world's richest cities in history and art, and one of Europe's greatest cultural, religious and intellectual centres. The two cultures of the Roman Empire and the Christian church give modern Rome her great monuments and churches and the immense riches of art and its religious importance make Rome one of the most visited cities of the world. In the year 2,000, it is expected that more than 30m. pilgrims will visit Rome. It is also a great centre of commerce with varied industries, such as printing, publishing, manufacturing, and motion pictures.

TRANSPORT

Airports
Most flights arrive at Leonardo da Vinci Airport (Fiumicino).
Tel: (0)6 65951

Connected by train to the Termini station in central Rome. Tickets can be purchased at the airport.

Some flights arrive at Ciampino Airport Tel: (0)6 79 49 41.
Connected by bus and subway to central Rome.

Trains

Stazione Termini: Tel: (0)6 4775

Most domestic, European and international rail services come into the main railway station.

Roads

Connected by motorways A1 (north/south), A12 (coastal north), A24 (west).

Buses

Rome has an efficient bus service (ATAC Tel: 167 555 666). Tickets must be bought before boarding and can be found at 'tabacchi', newspaper stands or at the main bus station at Stazione Termini (where most buses terminate).

Metropolitana (Subway)

Metro stations are marked M in red on a white square. Tickets are the same as for the bus and can be bought at tabacchi, news-stands, some bars, machines located in the stations and major bus stops.

Taxis

Taxis operate 24 hours. Can be found at taxi stands throughout the city, can be hailed or telephoned.

Cosmos Taxis. Tel: (0)6 988-177

Società Cooperativa Autoradio Taxi. Tel: (0)6 3570

Società La Capitale Radio Taxi. Tel: (0)6 4994

Scooter Hire

Motor scooters are an efficient (if sometimes scary) way of negotiating Rome traffic. They can be hired from:

Rent-a-Scooter, V. Filippo Turati, 50. Tel: (0)6 446-9222

Scooters for Rent, V. Della Purificazione, 84. Tel: (0)6 488-5485

Car Hire

Cars can be rented at airports, train stations and major hotels as well as at company locations.

See also central reservation numbers on page 168.

Main companies represented locally are:

AVIS: Fiumicino Airport. Tel: (0)6 6501-1579. Stazione Termini: (0)6 4701-219, toll free: 167 863-063

Dollarexpress: Vile delle Milizie 9d. Tel: (0)6 3751-5944, toll free: 167 865-110

Euronolo: Via Vialle Vermiglio 21. Tel: (0)6 8864-0185

Europcar: Fiumicino Airport. Tel: (0)6 6501-0879, Stazione Termini: (0)6 4882-854, Central: (0)6 5208-1200

Hertz: Fiumicino Airport. Tel: (0)6 6501-1448, Stazione Termini: (0)6 4740-389, toll free: 167 822-099

Maggiore: Fiumicino Airport. Tel: (0)6 6501-0678, Stazione Termini: (0)6 4880-049, toll free: 167 867-067

TRAVELLERS INFORMATION

Tourist Offices

Italian Government Tourist Board (ENIT):

Head Office: Via Marghera 2/6, 00185 Rome. Tel: (0)6 49711

Fax: (0)6 4463-379

Email: sedecentrale.enit@interbusiness.it

Web: www.enit.it

EPT (Provincial Tourist Office)

Central Office: V. Parigi 5. Tel: (0)6 4889-9255 or (0)6 4889-9253

Fax: (0)6 4889-9250

Offices also at Stazione Termini.

Information Websites

www.enit.it www.enjoyrome.com

www.initaly.com www.itwg.com

Post Office

Main post office: Piazza San Silvestro 28 (off Via del Tritone)

Financial and Currency

American Express: P. di Spagna, 38. Tel: (0)6 67641

Thomas Cook: P. Barberini, 21A. Tel: (0)6 4828-082

  Cash ATMs throughout the city or in banks.

Emergency

Police: Tel: 113 (English interpreter)

Carabinieri: Tel: 112 (Foreigners' Office for reporting thefts,

Tel: (0)6 4686-2711)

Fire: Tel: 113

Roadside assistance: Tel: 116

Crisis line: (Samaritans-English speaking) V. S. Giovanni in Laterano.

Tel: (0)6 7045-4444

Medical Emergency

First Aid: Tel: 118

Red Cross (Ambulance): Tel: (0)6 5510

Hospital: Rome-American Hospital: V.E. Longi 69. Tel: (0)6 2255-290

Policlinico Umberto 1: V. di Policlinico 155. (Tel: (0)6 2255-290 for

emergency or (0)6 722-551)

24 Hour Pharmacy: P. Barberini, 49. Tel: (0)6 485-456

Internet Access

Internet Café: V. dei Marrucini 12. Tel/fax: (0)6 4454-953

Email: info@internetcafe.it Web: www.internetcafe.it

Hackers: V. S. Veniero 10/16. Tel: (0)6 3973-9268
Email: hackers.2@flashnet.it

Hotel Reservations

See central reservation numbers on page 168.

Car Hire

See central reservation numbers on page 168.

Landmarks

(For Basilica di S. Pietro, Piazza S. Pietro (St. Peter's Church and Square), Museo Vaticano and the Capella Sistina (Vatican Museum and the Sistine Chapel) see under Vatican City on page 186).

The Roman Forum (Foro Romano), Imperial Forum (Fori Imperiali) and Palatine Hill (Palatino)

Reflecting 12 centuries of Roman history, the Roman Forum acted as the political, religious and commercial centre of ancient Rome. The forum as we see it today was excavated in the 19th and 20th centuries. The Forum is intersected by the Via Sacra, the oldest street in Rome, down which returning Roman Emperors marched in triumph to the Curia (the meeting place of the Senate). Among the many popular sights are the remains of temples, triumphal arches and municipal buildings. Legend has it that Romulus, the founder of Rome, is buried here beneath a flat grey stone between the Curia and the Rostrum. The three sacred trees of Rome – the olive, fig and grapevine – have been replanted nearby.

The Palatine Hill rises above the Roman Forum and is the place where legend has it that Romulus and Remus were discovered. The Farnesi Gardens, laid out in the 16th century on the site of Tiberius' palace, look out over the Forum and rest of Rome. The Imperial Forum sprawls across a site opposite the Roman Forum and contains the ruins of temples, basilicas and public squares constructed by the Emperors of the 1st and 2nd centuries.

The Coliseum (Colosseo): (M. Colosseo)

This vast amphitheatre with its superimposed classical orders (Doric, Ionic and Corinthian) was known as the Flavian Amphitheatre after Vespasian, the first of the Flavian Emperors who inaugurated it in AD 80. It was used as an arena for mock naval battles, gladiatorial contests and, more famously, for fights to the death between men and wild beasts. It was here that the Christians were fed to the lions. Now an integral part of the Coliseum, the Arch of Constantine, commemorating Constantine's victory over Maxentius in AD 315, leads the way to the Palatine Hill.

The Capitoline Hill (Campidoglio)

The Campidoglio was the most sacred part of Ancient Rome and now serves as the seat of the City Government. The municipal building is perched on a Piazza by Michelangelo. There are palaces and museums and beautiful gardens. The church of S. Pietro in Carcere, consecrated in part of the former Mamertine Prison, marks the spot where St. Peter (the first Pope and Bishop of Rome) is thought to have been imprisoned by the Romans.

Pantheon: (Piazza della Rotunda. Tel: (0)6 369-831)

This perfectly preserved ancient building started life as a temple. Originally built by Agrippa in 27 BC and rebuilt by Hadrian (117–125 AD) it was converted into a church in the 7th century. The enormous dome is a perfect half sphere supported only by a central oculus, which once gave all the light to the interior as well as supporting the dome. Mysteries of its construction have puzzled architects and archaeologists for centuries. The side chapels contain the tombs of the Kings of Italy and of the renaissance painter, Raphael. The Pantheon is situated in the centre of the most historic part of Rome (Centro Storico) and is reached through narrow winding streets.

Piazza Navona

The piazza was opened in 86 AD as a stadium hosting wrestling matches, javelin and discus throwing and chariot and foot races. It would also be flooded to stage mock naval battles. Not far from the Pantheon, the piazza is a pedestrianized space containing three fountains, with Bernini's masterpiece, the Fontana dei Quattro Fiumi (Fountain of the Four Rivers), at the centre. Bernini completed the fountain in 1651 and his four figures appear to be recoiling in horror at the sight of the façade of Chiesa di Sant'Agnese in Agonia built by his rival, Borromini. The square is surrounded by churches, palaces (including the Palazzo della Sapienza – the original home of the University of Rome) and, nowadays, pavement cafés and restaurants.

Piazza Barberini/ Palazzo Barberini /Museo Nazionale d'Arte
(National Museum of Art): (Via delle Quattro Fontane, 13.
Tel: (0)6 4814-591. M. Barberini)
The piazza has two famous fountains both by Bernini – the Fontana del Tritone, with the God Triton spouting water, and the Fontana delle Api, featuring the bees which are part of the coat of arms of the Barberini family. The Baroque Palace was built for the Barberini family by the combined talents of Boromini, Bernini and Maderno in the 17th century. It now houses the Museo Nazionale d'Arte – a magnificent art gallery devoted to paintings from the 11th to the 18th centuries by, among others, Lippi, Tintoretto, Caravaggio, Raphael, Titian, Holbein, etc.

The Via Vittorio Veneto (known as Via Veneto) runs off the Piazza with shops, cafés, airline offices and embassies. It was renowned during the 1960s for 'la dolce vita' and was the playground of Italian movie stars.

Villa Borghese

Just north of the Spanish Steps, this park was created by Scipione Borghese to celebrate his elevation to Cardinal. As well as the park and gardens, it also contains a zoo and three notable art museums.

Galleria Borghese. (Villa Borghese. Tel: (0)6 85477. M. Spagna) The Gallery is housed in the Palazzo Borghese and contains remarkable collections of sculptures by Canova and Bernini and paintings by Raphael, Correggio, Titian and Caravaggio.

Galleria Nazionale d'Arte Moderna. (Palazzo delle Belle Arte, V. Delle Belle Arte, 131, Villa Borghese. Tel: (0)6 322-981. M. Flaminio)

Houses a collection of Italian painting from the 19th century to the present day.

Museo Nazionale Etrusco: (P. Villa Giulia, 9 [Villa Borghese]. Tel: (0)6 3201-951)

Housed in the Villa Giulia – Pope Julius III's elegant 16th century 'country house' within the grounds of the Villa Borghese – the museum houses a fabulous collection of Etruscan artefacts including the famous sarcophagus adorned by sculptures of a man and his wife.

Basilica di San Giovanni in Laterano (Church of St. John the Lateran): The cathedral church of Rome, San Giovanni in Laterano is the oldest Christian Basilica in Rome. It was first begun by Constantine in 314 AD, rebuilt during the Baroque period by Borromini and altered again in the 18th century. The church houses some important relics – the heads of Saints Peter and Paul encased in golden reliquaries and the finger that the doubting Saint Thomas supposedly used to pierce Christ's wounds after his resurrection. The Lateran Palace was rebuilt in the 16th century and was the papal palace until the papal court returned from Avignon. The Scala Sancta is a vestige of the medieval palace and is said to be where Christ stood at his trial in the Palace of Pontius Pilate. Worshippers still climb the staircase on their knees to the papal chapel at the top.

Fontana di Trevi (Trevi Fountain)

This late Baroque extravaganza was commissioned from Nicolo Salvi by Pope Clement XIII in 1762 and depicts the ocean riding his chariot drawn by sea horses. Legend has it that the visitor to Rome will ensure a safe return to the city by throwing one coin into the fountain. Throwing two coins will ensure the granting of a wish and cause the thrower to fall hopelessly in love. Throwing yourself into the fountain will result in a hefty fine.

MILAN (MILANO):

City (1990 population, 1,449,403), capital of Lombardy, Northern Italy, in the Po basin.

Milan is believed to have been founded by Celtic tribes who settled along the Po River in the 7th century BC. Rome's legion marched into the area and occupied the town, naming it Mediolanum ('Middle of the Plain'). The town occupied a key position on the trade routes between Rome and North Western Europe and this ensured its growth and progressive prosperity. Charlemagne chose here to declare the freedom of Christians. The city endured centuries of invasions by barbarians until the 11th century when it became a free commune and rose to a position of leadership in Lombardy. The city-state was governed by a council drawn from all social classes. Despite increased prosperity, squabbles with neighbouring towns resulted in the Holy Roman Emperor laying siege to Milan in 1162. The city and its allies took revenge by forming the Lega Lombarda in 1176. From the mid-13th century, a succession of powerful families – the Torrianis, the Viscontis, and the Sforzas – ruled the city. These families created considerable wealth and power until, after passing to Spain in 1535, Milan passed to Austria under the Treaty of Utrecht in 1713 which ended the War of the Spanish Succession. In 1797, Napoleon made Milan the capital of his Cisalpine Republic and, five years later, of the Italian republic, crowning himself King of Italy there in 1805. After a short-lived occupation by Austria in 1814, the troops of Vittorio Emanuele II and Napoleon III defeated the Austrian forces at the Battle of Magenta and in 1859 Milan was incorporated into the new Kingdom of Italy. Milan today is a sprawling modern city. It was heavily bombed during World War II but the city was rebuilt and quickly grew to become the economic and financial heart of modern Italy, with textiles, machinery, chemicals and motor vehicles as the chief earners. Milan is also the centre of Italy's publishing, advertising, design and fashion industries.

TRANSPORT

Airports
Milan has two airports, Malpensa and Linate.
General flight information line for both airports: Tel: (0)2 7485-2200
Malpensa:
45 km from the centre of town. Intercontinental flights. AirPullman buses leave for the city centre every 30 minutes. Tel: (0)2 6698-4509
Linate:
7 km from town. Domestic, European and Intercontinental flights. STAM buses to centre of town leave every 20 minutes.
Tel: (0)2 717-106

Trains
General information line for all trains: Tel: 0147-888-088
Stazione Centrale. P. Duca d'Aosta. MM2/MM3 Stazione Centrale. Most mainline trains come in here.

Stazione Nord. Connects to Como, Erba and Varese.

Porta Genova. Lines to Vigevano, Alessandria and Asti.

Porta Garibaldi. Links Milan with Lecce and Valtellina (to the north-west).

Roads

Connections via motorways A1 (south), A4 (east/west), A8/A9 (north).

Buses

Intercity buses come into the Stazione Centrale.

Local Transport

Milan has a comprehensive Metro system (Milan Metro) and bus system (ATM). Information: Tel: 0167-016-857 or (0)2 4803-2403

Tickets can be bought from 'tabacchi', newsagents, tourist offices and stations (day, 2-day, weekly and/or monthly passes are available).

Taxis

Taxis operate 24 hours. Can be found at taxi stands throughout the city, can be hailed or telephoned.

Radio-taxi: Tel: (0)2 5353 or (0)2 8585 or (0)2 88383 or (0)2 5251

Car Hire

See central reservation numbers on page 168.

Hotel Reservations

See central reservation numbers on page 168.

TRAVELLERS INFORMATION

Tourist Office

APT. Palazzo di Turismo, V. Marconi, 1. Tel: (0)2 7252-4300

Fax: (0)2 7252-4350

Information Websites:

www.enit.it

www.initaly.com

www.itwg.com

Financial and Currency

American Express: V. Brera 3. Tel: (0)2 7200-3693

Currency exchanges and cash withdrawals at banks and cash ATMs.

Post Office

V. Cordusio, 4 (Near P. del Duomo). Tel: (0)2 8692-069

There are also two post offices in the Stazione Centrale.

Consulates

UK V. S. Paolo, 7. Tel: (0)2 723-001

USA V. P. Amadeo, 2/10. Tel: (0)2 2903-5141

For embassies, see under Diplomatic Representation on page 174.

Emergency

Police: Tel: 112 or (0)2 77271

Emergency Number: Tel: 113

Tourist Police: (SOS Touristica) V. Adige 11. Tel: (0)2 541-781

Medical Emergency

Ambulance: Tel: 118.

Pronto Soccorso: Tel: (0)2 3883.

Hospital: Ospedale Maggiore di Milano. V. Francesco Sforza 35.

Tel: (0)2 55031.

Late night pharmacy: Pharmacy in Stazione Centrale open 24hrs.

Night opening of pharmacies rotates.

Internet Access

Hard Disk Café. C. Sempione, 44. Tel: (0)2 3310-1038

Computers are also available in the basement of the Università Statale.

Ospedale Maggiore, V. Festa del Perdono.

Landmarks

Duomo (Cathedral)

The gothic Duomo, made of white marble and towering over the Piazza del Duomo, is the third largest church in Europe after St. Peter's in Rome and the Cathedral in Seville in Spain. The cathedral was founded in 1386 by Gian Galezzo Visconti in the hope that the Virgin Mary would grant him a male heir. It took over 400 years to build (Napoleon ordered the completion of the façade in 1809). It is adorned with over 3,400 statues, 96 gargoyles and several kilometres of stone tracery. The façade is a mixture of Gothic and Baroque styles and inside the five-aisled cruciform is supported by 52 columns.

Galleria Vittorio Emanuele

The Galleria extends from the Piazza del Duomo to the Piazza della Scala and is one of the most elegant (and one of the earliest) shopping malls in the world. Built in 1877 by Giuseppe Mangoni, the Gallery has mosaic floors, a vast glass barrel vaulted roof, and a glass cupola under which the 'Milanese' stroll, shop, and eat ice cream or sip coffee and aperitifs in the cafés.

Pinacoteca di Brera: (V. Brera 28. Tel (0)2 722-631. MM2: Lanza)

The Gallery is housed in a 17th century Palace and houses an impressive collection of paintings, including the largest and most important collection of the Venetian painters outside Venice. Most notable are the Monte Feltro altarpiece by Piero della Francesca, the Meal at Emmaus by Caravaggio, a Pietà by Bellini and the Dead Christ by Mantegna. There are sculpture rooms, a collection of paintings from the 19th and 20th centuries and the Jesi Collection – representing the main artistic movements of the first half of the 20th century.

Santa Maria delle Grazie: (P. di S. Maria delle Grazie and C. Magenta [off Via Carducci]. MM1: Conciliazione or MM2: Cadorno.
Tel: (0)2 4987-588)

The renaissance church was built by the Dominican religious order between 1465 and 1490 and was finished by Bramante. The interior (which has been restored) and impressive dome, gallery and cloister were all designed by Bramante. The former refectory of the Monastery (Cenacolo Vinciano) houses Leonardo da Vinci's fresco of The Last Supper. This most famous of Leonardo's works was commissioned by Ludovico il Moro in 1497 and because it was painted on the coldest wall in the room, the fresco has, over the centuries, deteriorated badly. In World War II the building was badly bombed – only the wall on which the fresco painted remained standing. The painting is permanently under some form of restoration. The Museo Nazionale della Scienza e Tecnica (V. San Vittore 21. Tel: 02-48-55-51. MM1: San Ambrogi) has exhibits devoted to the exploration of Leonardo's inventions and his works of art.

Teatro all Scala: (Piazza della Scala. Tel: (0)2 860-787 [Box office] Museo Teatrale all Scala. Tel: (0)2 8053-418)

Renowned as the world's most famous opera house, La Scala has presented productions with most of the famous names of Italian and international opera. Verdi and Toscanini both conducted at La Scala and it was here that Maria Callas made her name. The theatre was built between 1776 and 1778 on the site of a church – Chiesa di S. Maria alla Scala. The interior, which seats 2,000 people in six levels of boxes, is as elaborate and ornate as the Neo-classical exterior is simple. To see the theatre, enter through the Museo del Teatro where operatic memorabilia, including Verdi's top hat and casts of the hands of famous conductors can be seen.

Navigli District

The Neo-classical Arco di Porta Ticinese (built between 1801 and 1814) leads to the Navigli district of Milan. The medieval canal system (with footbridges designed by Leonardo da Vinci) was used to transport tons of marble to build the Duomo and linked Milan with the cities and lakes to the north. Known as the Venice of Lombardy, today this area has open-air markets, cafés, and narrow pedestrian alleyways.

TURIN (TORINO):

City (1990 population, 1,002,863), capital of Piedmont in north-west Italy.

The city stands at the confluence of the Dora Riparia and the Po rivers and is the crossroads of many of the most important transalpine routes from France and Switzerland. During the 1st century, the Taurinia made this city their capital (and gave it their name). In the early 5th century, the town converted to Christianity and became a bishopric. A century later, Turin was a Lombard duchy before passing under Frankish rule. From the beginning of the 11th century, Turin was linked to the house of Savoy, a dynasty that was to reign not only over Piedmont and Savoy but also, from 1720, Sardinia. Savoy was the reigning royal family of Italy from 1861 to 1946 and Turin was the capital of Italy from 1861 to 1865. The Savoys were skilful rulers, switching allegiance between the Popes and the Holy Roman

Emperors and playing France off against the Dukes of Milan. Their power and influence grew until in the 18th century Turin reached its peak of grandeur with a court, presided over by Charles Emmanuel II, similar in pomp and ceremony to that of Versailles. Many of the splendid buildings that we see today were built during this period. The French invaded Turin in 1798, expelling Charles Emmanuel II, but on the fall of Napoleon, Vittorio Emanuele was restored to his kingdom and made Turin the base for the struggle for a unified Italy. In the latter part of the 18th century, Camillo Cavour (architect of the Risorgimento – the movement for the unification of Italy) reorganized Piedmont. After the success of the Franco-Piedmontese allied campaigns against the Austrians when Vittorio Emanuele II was proclaimed King of Italy, Turin became the seat of the Italian government. The House of Savoy reigned over Italy until the proclamation of the Italian Republic in 1946. During World War II, Turin was heavily bombed. After 1946 it became the main industrial centre and the focus for the Italian Trade Union movement. Turin's giants of industry, among them Olivetti, Fiat (founded by the powerful Agnelli family) and Lancia, have given rise to other manufacturing industries such as tyre-making and coach-building (most famously Pinin Farina). The Politecnico at Turin University produces most of the motor industry's engineers. Turin was also the birthplace of Italian cinema, with Pietro Fosco shooting his silent film 'Cabiria' on the banks of the Po in 1914. As well as being Italy's second largest industrial city (after Milan) and a bustling commercial centre, the city of Turin is an elegant city with graceful arcaded avenues, spacious squares, and innumerable palaces and churches.

TRANSPORT

Airport

Castelle Airport. Tel: (0)11 5676-361 or (0)11 5676-362

Domestic and European flights.

Connected to the centre of Turin by bus. SADEM bus company.
Tel: (0)11 3111-616

Trains

Porta Nuova. C. Vittorio Emanuele. Tel: (0)11 5613-333

The city's main railway station with services to Paris, Milan, Venice,
Genoa and Rome.

Roads

Connected by motorways A5 (north), A4 (east to Milan and Venice),
A21 (south-east) A6 (south).

Buses

Trasporti Torinesi. Tel: (0)11 538-376

The city is served by a network of buses and trams. There is an
information booth in the Stazione Porta Nuova. Tickets valid for both
bus and tram can be bought at 'tabacchi'.

Taxis

Taxis operate 24 hours. Can be found at taxi stands throughout the
city, can be hailed or telephoned.

Radio Cabs: (0)11 5737, (0)11 5730 or (0)11 3399

Bicycle Hire

Parco Valentino Noleggio Biciclette, V. Mattioli, Parco Valentino.

Car Hire

See central reservation numbers on page 168.

TRAVELLERS INFORMATION

Tourist Office
APT: P. Castello (corner of Via Roma). Tel: (0)11 535-181 or
(0)11 535-901
Smaller office at the Porta Nuova railway station. Tel: (0)11 531-327
Information Websites: www.enit.it www.initaly.com www.itwg.com

Post Office
Main Post Office: Via Alfieri 10. Postal code 10100. Tel: (0)11 535-894
or (0)11 5628-100

Financial and Currency
American Express (at the airport): Tel: (0)11 567-697
   Cash ATMs throughout the city. Banks located along Via Roma.

Emergency
Police: C. Vinzaglio. Tel: 112 or (0)11 55881
Fire: Tel: 113

Medical Emergency
First Aid: Tel: (0)11 5080-370
Ambulance: Tel: 118 or (0)11 280-333
Hospital: Maurizio Umberto, L. Turati 62. Tel: (0)11 5080-111
24 hours Pharmacy: Farmacia Boniscontro, C. Vittorio Emanuele, 66.
Tel: (0)11 541-271 or (0)11 538-271

Internet Access
Transpan Cyber Service. C. Vittorio Emanuele, 12B.
Tel: (0)11 885-512 Fax: (0)11 8177-822 Email: transpan@transpan.it

Hotel Reservations
See central reservation numbers on page 168.

Landmarks

Duomo di S. Giovanni: (Tel: (0)11 4361-540)
Turin's cathedral contains one of the most famous relics of Christianity, the Shroud of Turin (in which the body of Christ was said to have been wrapped before his entombment and which apparently bears the imprint of his body). Enclosed within a silver vessel in the Capella della Santa Sindone (Chapel of the Holy Shroud) beneath the black marble dome built by Guarini between 1668 and 1694, the Shroud attracts millions of visitors each year.

Mole Antonelliana: (V. Montebello 20)
This landmark and symbol of Turin started life as a synagogue. Reached by glass elevator the site affords a stunning panorama of the city. There are plans to move the Museo Nazionale del Cinema from the Palazzo Madama in the centre of Turin to this site.

Museo dell'Automobile: (Corso Unità d'Italia 40)
Reflecting Turin's long association with the motor industry, the museum houses a remarkable collection of cars in a vast modern building, including one of the first Fiats and the Isotta Franchini driven by Gloria Swanson in Sunset Boulevard. There is also an extensive library and archive and there is even a room devoted to the history of tyre manufacture.

Palazzo Reale: (Piazza Castello. Tel: (0)11 4361-455)
The Princes of the House of Savoy lived in this Palace from 1645 until 1865. It was built for Carlo Emanuele II in 1645 with a deceptively plain exterior concealing the elaborate red and gold Baroque apartments inside. There is a collection of Chinese vases and the gardens were designed in 1697 by Le Nôtre (famous for his gardens at Versailles).

Armorio Reale: (P. Castello 191. Tel: (0)11 543-889)
In one wing of the Palazzo Reale the Armorio Reale houses one of the world's best collections of medieval and renaissance arms and armour.

Palazzo Carignano

The Palazzo Carignano with its impressive Baroque façade was built by Guarini in 1680, and was the birthplace of King Vittorio Emanuele II, the first King of Italy, in 1820. It now contains the Museo Nazionale del Risorgimento Italiano with a fascinating collection of historic documents and political memorabilia of Italy in the 19th century. The Palace acted as the Chamber for Italy's first parliament.

GENOA (GENOVA):

City (1990 population, 706,754), capital of Liguria, Northwest Italy.

Genoa was founded in the 4th century BC and was a key Roman port. The city grew rapidly into a powerful mercantile centre albeit under a variety of foreign occupying powers. Genoa was occupied by the French in 774, the Saracens in the 10th century and by the Milanese in 1353. A long rivalry existed with the other great northern Italian maritime power, Venice, as they fought for control over the valuable Mediterranean trading routes. By the end of the 14th century, despite years of strife between three noble families (the Grimaldis, the Dorias and the Spinolas), Genoa was a very prosperous city state with colonies as far afield as the Black Sea. In the 16th century, Admiral Andrea Doria's enterprising and independent spirit led Genoa into an era of military and political successes. He drew up a new aristocratic constitution, which gave Genoa the status of a mercantile republic. While the renaissance was sweeping Italy, Genoa entered a golden age that lasted well into the 17th century. Magnificent palaces were built, and artists like Rubens, Caravaggio and van Dyck were attracted to work in the city. The architect Galezeo Alessi designed and built many of the city's most splendid buildings. In the 18th century, the decline in the importance of the

Mediterranean as a trading route affected Genoa, but by the middle of the 19th century, under the leadership of Giuseppe Mazzini, Genoa was at the forefront of the cause for the unification of Italy – the Risorgimento. A century later, at the end of World War II, the people of Genoa led the rise against the Germans and the Italian Fascists and liberated their own city before the arrival of the Allied troops. After a period of boom in the 1960s, port activity declined and with it the fortunes of the city. The port and the waterfront fell into disrepair and the city centre showed signs of neglect. In 1992, however, the Columbus Festival attracted huge incoming investment and the now largely privatized port operations are handling increasingly large amounts of container business. Genoa is now Italy's chief port handling heavy passenger as well as freight traffic. Iron and steel, chemicals, oil refineries and shipyards still lead the economy, but the service sector is increasingly important. Famous sons of Genoa include the explorer and discoverer of America, Christopher Columbus, and the violinist, Paganini.

TRANSPORT

Airport
Cristoforo Colombo Internazionale: Sestre Ponente (6 km west of the city). Tel: (0)10 60151. Flight info: Tel: (0)10 2411

Domestic and European flights and international connections.

Connected to the Stazione Brignole and Stazione Principe in Genoa by bus.

Volabus: (0)10 599-414

Trains
Genoa has two main railway stations both providing domestic and international services.

Stazione Principe: P. Aquaverde.

Stazione Brignole. P. Verdi. Tel: (0)10 284-081 (train information for both stations).

Roads

Connected by motorways: A7 (north to A21) and A12 (Coastal route north/south)

Buses

International and long distance buses arrive in Piazza della Vittoria.

Local transport

Buses operate throughout Genoa.

ATM. V. d'Annunzio 8r. Tel: (0)10 5997-414

Tickets and one-day tourist passes (with foreign passport) are available from tourist offices.

Ferries

Genoa's ferry lines provide passenger services to other ports along the coast, as well as to Sardinia, Corsica, Sicily, etc.

Boats arrive and depart from the Stazione Marittima.

Tel: (0)10 256-682

Grandi Traghetti: Tel: (0)10 589-331 or (0)10 5761-363 (Palermo)

Tirrenia: Tel: (0)10 2758-041 (Porto Torres, Sardinia)

Corsica Ferries, Sardinia Ferries and Elba Ferries.

Tel: (0)10 593-301 or (0)10 5531-000 Fax: (0)10 593-774

Taxis

Taxis operate 24 hours. Can be found at taxi stands throughout the city, can be hailed or telephoned.

Radio cabs: Tel: (0)10 5966

TRAVELLERS INFORMATION

Tourist Offices

APT. Porto Antico, Palazzina S. Maria. Tel: (0)10 24871

Fax: (0)10 2467-658

Branches at Via Roma 11 (2nd floor) Tel: (0)10 576-791, Stazione Principe. Tel: (0)10 2462-633, Cristoforo Colombo Airport. Tel: (0)10 6015-247

Information Websites: www.enit.it www.initaly.com www.itwg.com

Consulates

UK P. della Vittoria 15. Tel: (0)10 5531-516

USA V. Dante 2. Tel: (0)10 584-492

Post Office

Main Post Office. Piazza Dante 4r. (off Piazza de Ferrari). Tel: (0)10 2594-687

Financial and Currency

Many banks to be found around P. Corvetto. Exchange (Cambio) at the railway stations. ATMs throughout the city.

Emergency

Police: Tel: 122

Other emergency: Tel: 113

Carabinieri: Via Diaz. Tel: (0)10 53661.

Medical Emergency

Ambulance: Tel: 118.

Medical emergency. Tel: 113.

Hospital: Ospedale San Martino, V. Benedetto XV 10. Tel: (0)10 5551

24 hour Pharmacy: V. Balbi 185r (Near Stazione Principe). Tel: (0)10 2462-697 or (0)10 252-786 or (0)10 256-921

Internet Access

Bancamed Sri. V.S. Vincenzo 101r. Tel: (0)10 540-035.

Landmarks

Galleria Nazionale/Palazzo Spinola: (P. Pellicceria 1.

Tel: (0)10 2477-061)

The palace, once the home of the Spinola family, was built in the 16th and 17th centuries and is also the home of the Galleria Nazionale with collections of paintings housed in beautifully decorated rooms. The ceilings are decorated with frescoes by Tavarone, Ferrari and Galeotti, and artists include Antonello da Messina, Joos van Cleve, van Dyck and Breughel the Younger.

Via Garibaldi

The Street of Palaces, once named Via Aurea and known as Strada dei Re (Street of the Kings), was built to the designs of Alessi in the 16th century. On either side of the street are elegant palaces that once housed the great families of Genoa. Palazzo Cambiaso (number 1), Palazzo Parodi (number 3) and Palazzo Carrega-Cataldi (number 4) are all by Alessi, the latter having a delightful entrance and gilded gallery. Palazzo Doria (number 6) and Palazzo Podestà are by the architect Castello. The Palazzo Municipale (the town hall at number 9) has a beautiful arcaded courtyard and houses a collection with, among other things, a violin of Paganini and manuscripts by Christopher Columbus. The Palazzo Bianco (number 11) contains a fine art gallery with Flemish, Dutch, French and Spanish works. Painters include Provost, Van der Goes, David, van Dyck and Rubens.

Palazzo Rosso (number 18) houses works by the Venetian artists Titian, Veronese and Tintoretto and fine examples of the Genoese school of painting, as well as a canvas by Dürer and some portraits by van Dyck.

Via Balbi/Palazzo Reale

Here there is another magnificent street of palaces. Among the most notable is the Palazzo Reale (number 10), formerly the Palazzo Balbi Durazzo, which dates from 1650 and contains a van Dyck room. The imposing Palazzo del'Università (number 5) dates from the 17th century and has a grand elegant staircase and courtyard. Palazzo Durazzo Pallavicini (number 1) dates from the 17th century.

Duomo di San Lorenzo

Built between the 12th and 16th centuries, the splendid gothic façade of the Cathedral is a perfect example of the Genoese style. French influence can be seen in the 13th century doorways and the large rose window. The Capella di San Giovanni Battista has statues of Adam and Eve by Mateo Civitali and allegedly contains the bones of St. John the Baptist. The Treasury contains the famous Sacro Catino – the cup that, according to legend, is the Holy Grail.

Acquario

This magnificent aquarium is Europe's largest and is a leftover from the Columbus exhibition of 1992. Sharks, dolphins, reptiles, seals and penguins are visible in a series of modern well-designed environments. The visit begins with an introductory film followed by a computerized system of instruction that gives the visitor an opportunity for a 'hands on' experience as they walk through reconstructions of the underwater worlds of the Mediterranean and the Red Sea, a tropical forest and a coral reef. Next door to the aquarium is 'Il Bigo', an enormous derrick that hoists the visitor up 200 metres in a cylindrical lift for a bird's eye view of the city and the waterfront.

NAPLES (NAPOLI):

City (1990 population, 1,204,149), capital of Campania, southern central Italy, on the Bay of Naples.

Legend has it that the siren Parthenope gave her name to the original settlement that grew up around her tomb but Phoenician traders and Athenian Greeks who settled there a thousand years later renamed it Neapolis (the new city). It rapidly prospered as a centre of Greek and Roman culture, the latter co-exisitng with the Greek language and influence. Rich inhabitants of Rome like Pompey, Caesar, Virgil, Nero and Tiberius all favoured Naples as the place to spend the winter. Since the 12th century, a succession of princely families has ruled Naples. The Normans were overthrown by the Hohenstaufens in 1139. The Swabian dynasty of the Hohenstaufens, which lasted until 1266, gave Naples many new institutions including the University. The Angevins under Charles I, having taken Sicily, defeated the last of the Hohenstaufens and made Naples the de facto capital. After a period of uprising and disorder, Naples came under the rule of the Spanish house of Aragon. Alfonso I introduced new laws, a modern concept of justice and promoted the arts and sciences. When Naples (and the kingdom of Sicily) were absorbed into the Spanish Empire a series of Spanish viceroys ruled the city as virtual dictators. But Naples continued to flourish and the rule of the Spanish Bourbons re-established Naples as the capital of the Kingdom of the Two Sicilies in 1734. Apart from a short period between 1806 and 1815 when Naples came under Napoleonic France (first under Joseph Napoleon, Emperor Napoleon Bonaparte's brother and then under Joachim Murat) the Bourbons remained the rulers of Naples. Despite a couple of uprisings, they retained power until the arrival of Garibaldi and the Kingdom of Italy in 1860, when the city was a serious contender to become the new nation's capital.

Naples was heavily bombed in World War II and it is thought that the struggle to reorganize and rebuild the damaged city contributed to the post war boom in organized crime. The city suffered a major earthquake in 1980 and the close proximity of Vesuvius, a dormant but not extinct volcano, continues to threaten the city. Naples today is a crowded, noisy city; it is a major seaport and a commercial and industrial centre. Renowned for its castles, palaces, cathedrals and museums, the present municipal government has undertaken an aggressive restoration programme of the city's art treasures. This, and the success of the programme to reduce crime, has resulted in a dramatic increase in the city's tourist industry.

TRANSPORT

Airport

Capodichino Airport. (5 km north of the city). V. Umberto Maddalena. Tel: (0)81 7896-111

Connected to P. Municipio in Naples by airport buses. CPL. Tel: (0)81 5311-706

Trains

Stazione Centrale. Piazza Garibaldi. Tel: (0)81 5543-188

The city is served by regional, national and international trains and most of them arrive and depart from the Stazione Centrale.

Local trains

Circumvesuviana: Tel: (0)81 7722-444. Services to Pompeii, Herculaneum and Sorrento.

Ferrovia Cumana and Ferrovia Circumflegrea: Tel: (0)81 5513-328. Services to Pozzuoli, Baia and Cumae.

Roads

Connected by motorways A1 (north/south) and A16 (east).

Buses

National and International buses arrive and depart from the Piazza
Garibaldi in front of the Stazione Centrale.

SITA: Tel: (0)81 5522-176

CLP: Tel: (0)81 5311-706

Local Transport

Naples has a network of buses, trains (see local trains above), metro
and funicular ATAN (city buses and trams). One ticket is valid for all
forms of city transport and can be bought from ATAN booths and
'tabacchi'.

Trams go along the coast and depart near Stazione Centrale.

Funiculars go up into the Vomero hills and the main line leaves from
Piazza Fugo on Via Roma.

Ferries

Ferries and hydrofoils serve Capri, Sorrento, Ischia, Procida, Forio,
Casmicciola, Palermo, Cagliari, Milazzo and the Aeolian Islands.
They leave from either Stazione Marittima or Stazione Mergellina.

SNAV. Via Caracciolo 10. Tel: (0)81 7612-348 (Capri, Procida and
Ischia)

Alilauro. Via Caracciolo 11. Tel: (0)81 7611-004 (Ischia and
Sorrento)

Caremar. Molo Beverello. Tel: (0)81 5513-882 (Capri, Ischia and
Procida)

Navigazione Libera del Golfo. Tel: (0)81 5527-209 (Capri and
Sorrento)

Tirrenia. Tel: (0)81 5512-181 (Palermo and Cagliari – with connections to Trapani and Tunisia)

Siremar. Tel: (0)81 7613-688 (Aeolian Islands and Milazzo)

Linea Lauro. Tel: (0)81 5513-352 (Trapani and Tunis and, in high season, Sardinia and Corsica)

Taxis

Taxis operate 24 hours. Can be found at taxi stands throughout the city, can be hailed or telephoned.

Radio Cabs: Napoli: Tel: (0)81 5564-444; Cotana: Tel: (0)81 5707-070

TRAVELLERS INFORMATION

Tourist Offices

EPT: Tel: (0)81 268-779

Main office. P. Martiri, 58. Tel: (0)81 405-311

Stazione Mergellina. Tel: (0)81 7805-761

Information Websites:

www.enit.it

www.initaly.com

www.itwg.com

Consulates

UK V. Crispi 122. Tel: (0)81 663-511

USA U Piazza delle Repubblica (West End of Villa Communale).

Tel: (0)81 5838-111

24 hour emergency: Tel: 0337 945-083

Post Office

Main Post Office: Piazza G. Matteo (off Via A. Diaz).

Tel: (0)81 5511-456

Finance and Currency

Thomas Cook: Piazza Municipio 70. Tel: (0)81 5518-399

American Express. (Every Tour) Piazza Municipio 5.

Tel: (0)81 518-564

Stazione Centrale has 24 hours currency exchange or cash ATMs throughout the city.

Emergency

Police: Tel: 113 or (0)81 7941-111 (English spoken)

Carabinieri: Tel: 112

Other emergency: Tel: 113

Medical Emergency

Ambulance: Tel: (0)81 7520-696

Hospital: Cardarelli (North of Naples on the R4 bus line).

Tel: (0)81 7471-111

24 hours Pharmacy: Stazione Centrale (by the ticket windows).

Tel: (0)81 268-881

One pharmacy in each area stays open all night. See Il Mattino newspaper for lists.

Internet Access

Internetbar. P. Bellini, 74. Tel: (0)81 295-237

Internet Café. V. Giancardo Tramontano 12. Tel: (0)81 281-863.

Email: icafe@mds.it. Web: www.mds.it/cafe

Landmarks

Museo Archeologica Nazionale: (Piazza Cavour. Tel: (0)81 440-166) This museum is housed in a 16th century building originally intended for the royal cavalry. It then became the seat of the University from 1610 to 1777. Charles of Bourbon created the museum in the 18th century to display the rich collection of antiquities he had inherited from his mother, Elizabeth Farnese. The palace also houses the Borgia collection of Etruscan and Egyptian relics. Most of the Farnese collection is found on the ground floor and includes the vast Farnese Bull. This sculpture of a group depicting the death of Dirce is carved from a single block of marble. It is a Roman copy of a Greek sculpture and dates from the 2nd century BC. It was later restored by Michelangelo. The first floor is largely devoted to discoveries from Pompeii, Herculaneum, Stabae and Cumae. There are murals and frescoes, gladiators' helmets, household items, ceramics and glassware all rescued from archaeological sites. On the mezzanine there is a gallery of mosaics, including the wall-sized Battle of Alexander that once paved the floor of the Casa del Fauno at Pompeii.

Palazzo and Galleria Nazionale di Capodimonte: (to the north of Naples near Piazza Museo. Tel: (0)81 7441-307)

Surrounded by extensive gardens, this former royal estate commands the high ground to the north of Naples. The massive palace was built between 1738 and 1838 by Charles Bourbon, and the gallery now houses, among other things, another great Farnese family collection. The collections feature works by such artists as Titian, Goya, Botticelli, Caravaggio, Michelangelo, Masacchio and Lippi. There are also examples of the Florentine and Siennese Schools and an impressive number of 18th century Neapolitan paintings. The museum is housed in the royal apartment and includes collections of arms, ivories, bronzes and porcelain (including over 3,000 pieces from the palace's own porcelain factory).

Spaccanapoli

Following the course of an old Roman road, Decimanus Maximus, through the oldest part of Naples, Spaccanapoli (meaning streets that bisect Naples) refers to a maze of ancient streets with numerous churches, dilapidated palaces, small craft studios, cafés and shops. The three main streets are Via Benedetto Croce, Via San Biagio dei Libri and Via Vicaria Vecchia. Walking through these streets it is possible to trace the city's history from Graeco-Roman times to the present.

Certosa di San Martino: (off Corso Vittorio Emanuele.
Tel: (0)81 5781-769)
Built in the 14th century as a Carthusian Monastery, it was rebuilt in the 17th century by Fanzango in Neapolitan Baroque style and now houses the Museo Nazionale di San Martino. The building is overlooked by the Castel Sant'Elmo to the west. Fanzango also designed the cloisters. The lavishly decorated Baroque interior of the monastery's church contains works by Caracciolo, Guido Rein and Simon Vouet. The monastery itself has been converted into a museum chronicling the art history and life of Naples through the ages.

Palazzo Reale and Museo del Palazzo Reale: (Piazza del Plebiscito.
Tel: (0)81 5808-111)
  The royal palace was built at the beginning of the 17th century by Domenico Fontana. The façade retains most of its original Neoclassical features although it has been remodelled several times. Statues of the eight most important kings of Italy were inserted in niches in the façade in 1888. The museum is housed in the royal apartments (which were only inhabited by royalty after 1714) and the rich collections of furnishings, tapestries, statues and paintings vividly illustrate how the Bourbon rulers of Naples lived in the 19th century. The Palazzo Reale also houses the Biblioteca Nazionale, which contains more than 1·5m. volumes.

Teatro San Carlo: (Palazzo Reale, Piazza del Plebiscito.
Tel: (0)81 7972-331)
  Charles Bourbon originally commissioned the building of this theatre in 1737 but it was rebuilt in the Neo-classical style in 1816. It is the largest and one of the most distinguished opera theatres in

Italy. It has a splendid auditorium with boxes on six levels and is built entirely of wood and stucco to achieve perfect acoustics. The opera house is an important institution in the Italian music world.

PALERMO:

Palermo (1990 population, 731,418) is the capital, largest city, and chief port of Sicily.

Palermo's superb (and strategic) seaside position on the island of Sicily – at the foot of Monte Pellegrino, with the fertile Conca d'Oro valley behind – has made the city irresistible to colonizers over the centuries.

Founded in the 6th century BC by the Phoenicians, it became a Carthaginian base, was taken by Rome in 153 BC and in the 6th century fell under Byzantium. From 831 to 1072 it was under the control of the Saracens. Palermo flourished under Arab rule and much of the city's present character, architectural influence and atmosphere date from this period. When the Normans invaded and took control in 1072, Roger II took the title of King of Sicily. He embarked on an ambitious programme of building, which succeeded in blending the Norman style of architecture with the decorative traditions of Byzantium and the Saracens. His reign was the golden age of art in Palermo, hailed as one of the most magnificent and cultured cities of 12th century Europe. The monarchy passed to the Hohenstaufens then to the Angevin French. Charles I of Anjou was the brother of the French King Louis IX and although he ruled Sicily with support of the Pope he was unpopular. In 1282, some young women of Palermo were insulted by a Frenchman (just as the bells were ringing for Vespers) and this sparked off the uprising known as the Sicilian Vespers. In the ensuing chaos, all Frenchmen who could not pronounce the word Cicero (chickpea) were massacred. By now, Sicily's power was eclipsed by Naples. Palermo began to decline in power and influence. In the years between the two world wars, Sicily became known as the power centre of the Mafia. Since World War II (during which Palermo was heavily bombed) great efforts have been made to curb the Mafia's power and many trials have taken place of people accused of having dealings with the Mafia. Along with its political clean up, the city is tackling the restoration of its historic and architectural treasures. Palermo produces citrus fruits from the Conca d'Oro valley and manufactures textiles, processed food and ships.

TRANSPORT

Airport
Cinisi-Punta-Raisi Airport. Tel: (0)91 6019-333 (domestic) or (0)91 7020-111 (international)
   Connected to P. Ruggero Settimo in Palermo by public (blue) buses or by taxi.

Trains
Stazione Centrale. Piazza Cesare. Tel: (0)91 6161-806
   Trains depart and arrive at the Stazione Centrale. There are services to cities and towns on the island of Sicily as well as Intercity trains to Reggio Calabria, Naples and Rome.

Roads
Connected by motorways A19 (to A20 east) and A19 (to A29 west).

Buses
International and long distance buses arrive and depart from the Intercity bus station at Via Paolo Balsamo.

Cuffaro: V. Paolo Balsamo 13. Tel: (0)91 6160-1510

Segesta: V. Balsamo 26. Tel: (0)91 6167-919

SAIS. V. Balsamo 16. Tel: (0)91 6166-028

Local Transport

The city is serviced by orange city buses.

AMAT. V. A. Borelli 14. Tel: (0)91 321-333. Tickets may be bought at booths at the terminal or from 'tabacchi'.

There is also a modest Metro system with 10 stations radiating out from the Stazione Centrale.

Ferries

Ferries arrive at and depart from Molo Vittorio Veneto off Via Francesco Crispi. There are services to Cagliari (Sardinia), Naples, Livorno, Genoa, the Aeolian Islands, Ustica, Malta and Tunisia. The service to Tunisia goes via Malta with a 19-hour stopover.

Tirrenia: Calata Marinai d'Italia. Off Via Francesco Crispi. Tel: (0)91 333-300 (Sardinia, Naples, Livorno and Genoa).

Siremar: Via Francesco Crispi 118. Tel: (0)91 582-403 (Ustica and the Aeolian Islands)

SNAV. (Pietro Barbaro Agency). Via Principe Belmonte 55. Tel: (0)91 333-333 (Aeolian Islands)

Grandi Traghetti. Via Mariano Stabile 57. Tel: (0)91 587-404 (Genoa, Malta and Tunisia)

TRAVELLERS INFORMATION

Tourist Offices

APT: Piazza Castelnuovo 34. Tel: (0)91 6058-351 or (0)91 6058-111 (Main office).

There are two smaller offices at the Stazione Marittima and the Piazza San Sepolcro.

Assessorato Communale Turismo: Toll free telephone information about local events: Tel: 167 234-169

Information Websites: www.enit.it   www.initaly.com www.itwg.com

Consulates

UK V.C. Cavour 177. Tel: (0)91 326-412

USA V. Re Frederico 18 (off Viale della Libertà).

Tel: (0)91 6110-020

Post Office

Main Post Office: V. Roma 322. Tel: (0)91 160 or (0)91 6959-111

Financial and Currency

American Express (G. Ruggieri & Figli). V.E. Amari 40.

Tel: (0)91 587-144

Exchange at the Stazione Centrale (Information window).

Banks and Cash ATMs throughout the city.

Emergency

Police: Tel: 113

The Questura (to report crimes). Tel: (0)91 210-111

Roadside assistance. Tel: 116

Ambulance. Tel: (0)91 306-644

Hospital: Policlinico Universitario. Tel: (0)91 6553-727 or Villa Sofia.

Tel: (0)91 7808-111

First Aid: Tel: (0)91 6662-201

24 hour Pharmacy: Lo Cascio, Via Roma 1. Tel: (0)91 6162-117 (near the Stazione Centrale)

Landmarks

Palazzo dei Normanni: (Corso Vittorio Emanuele)
Also known as the Palazzo Reale, this is now the seat of Sicily's
regional government. The original 9th century Moorish fortress was
extended by the Normans and restructured by the Hohenstaufens.
The Chapel (Cappella Palatina) was built in the reign of the Norman
king, Roger II, between 1130 and 1140 and is a superb example of
Arab-Norman decoration and design. Ten ancient columns support
horseshoe-shaped arches and the dome and apses are covered
with dazzling mosaics (second only to Ravenna and Constantinople
in magnificence). The carved wooden ceiling has a Moorish
'stalactite' design. On the floor above, the Sala di Ruggero is
adorned with 12th century mosaics depicting all manner of flora and
fauna.

The Duomo: (Via Papireto)
The Normans founded the cathedral, built in Sicilian-Norman style, at
the end of the 12th century. Over the centuries it has been modified
and added to – especially the south porch in the 15th century and
the Dome in the 18th century. In the 18th century, the interior was
altered, with only the apse retaining its original Norman style. Despite
obvious Moorish influences, the interior is in the Neo-classical style.
The cathedral houses the tombs of Emperor Frederick II as well as
past rulers of Sicily from the houses of Hohenstaufen, Anjou and
Aragon.

Museo delle Marionette: (V. Butera 1. Tel: (0)91 328-060)
Sicily has a lively tradition of puppet shows and in the past these
animated musical plays were an important part of Sicilian life. The
plots were usually stories of chivalry featuring two characters,
Rinaldo and Orlando. The puppets of Gaspare Canino – Sicily's
illustrious 19th century puppet-maker – are amongst the oldest in
the collection, which includes puppets from all over the world.

Piazza Pretoria

On the south side of this graceful square is the Palazzo del Municipio, also known as the Palazzo dell Aquile, because of the sculptures of eagles guarding each corner of the roof. On the East Side is the Chiesa di Santa Caterina. The centre of the square is occupied by a spectacular fountain (Fontana Pretoria), sculpted by Florentine artists in the 16th century. When it was unveiled, the shocked local people named it the Fountain of Shame because of the many nude marble statues that surmount it.

Teatro Massimo: (Piazza Giuseppe Verdi)

The theatre was constructed in the Neo-classical style between 1875 and 1897. It boasts the second largest indoor stage in Europe (after the one in the Paris Opera House) and the lavish interior has an opulent rotunda at its centre. Why the restoration of this important building has taken 20 years has been a source of much speculation but it is thought that the theatre will reopen in the year 2000. Meanwhile, the opera company and symphony orchestra give performances in another glittering gold and red room in the theatre.

San Giovanni degli Eremite: (V. dei Bendettini 3.)

Built in 1132 during the reign of Roger II by Norman and Moorish architects working together, the church is a perfect example of the mixture of styles that goes to make up so much of Palermo's architectural heritage. Topped by extravagant pink domes, the church stands in tranquil gardens surrounded by an elegant 13th century cloister that provides a peaceful and romantic resting-place.

SWITZERLAND
AUSTRIA
HUNGARY
FRANCE
Bolzano
TRENTINO-
ALTO ADIGE
Calalzo
FRIULI-
VENEZIA
GIULIA
SLOVENIA
Aosta
Como
Sondrio
Bergamo
Trento
Belluno
Udine
Trieste
CROATIA
VALLE
D'AOSTA
Novara
Milan
Brescia
Verona
VENETO
Vicenza
Padua
Venice
Vercelli
LOMBARDY
Turin
Asti
Pavia
Cremona
Alessandria
Piacenza
Mantua
Ferrara
BOSNIA
HERZEGOVINA
PIEMONTE
Parma
Modena
Savona
Genoa
EMILIA-
Bologna
ROMAGNA
Monte
Carlo
LIGURIA
Ravenna
Ventimiglia
La Spezia
Faenza
Rimini
N
Viareggio
Lucca
Florence
Pesaro
Pisa
Urbino
MARCHE
Ancona
Livorno
Arezzo
Cortona
Macerata
Siena
Elba
TUSCANY
Perugia
Grosseto
UMBRIA
Ascoli
Piceno
Terni
Pescara
Corsica
(Fr.)
Viterbo
Rieti
L'Aquila
ADRIATIC
SEA
LAZIO
ABRUZZO
Civitavecchia
Rome
MOLISE
Campobasso
Foggia
Porto
Torres
Olbia
Formia
CAMPANIA
Benevento
Bari
Brindisi
Sassari
Naples
Potenza
PUGLIA
Salerno
Matera
Lecce
SARDINIA
TYRRHENIAN
SEA
BASILICATA
Taranto
Cagliari
Iglesias
Ustica
Cosenza
CALABRIA
Catanzaro
Lipari Islands
Reggio di
Calabria
Palermo
Messina
IONIAN
SEA
Egadi Islands
Trapani
Enna
SICILY
Catania
Mazara
del Vallo
Agrigento
Ragusa
Syracuse
ITALY
TUNISIA
Pantelleria

National boundary
Province boundary

0   100 km

Map © Rough Guides Ltd, 1999

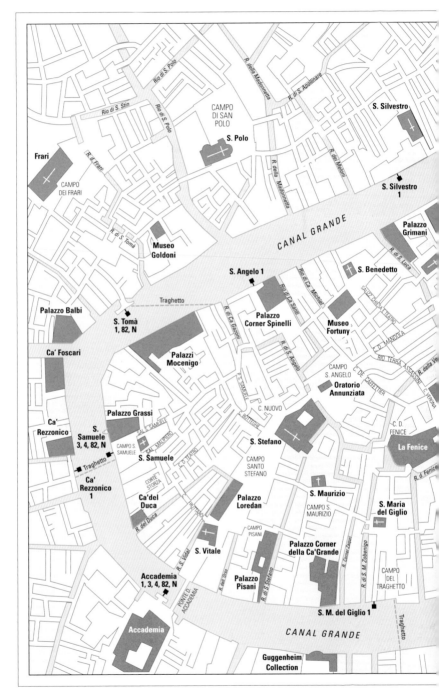

CAMPO DI SAN POLO

S. Silvestro

S. Polo

S. Silvestro 1

Frari

CAMPO DEI FRARI

Rio di S. Stin

Rio di S. Polo

R. di S. Polo

R. di S. Polo

R. d. Frari

R. della Madonnetta

R. di S. Apollinare

R. dei Meloni

R. della Madonnetta

CANAL GRANDE

Palazzo Grimani

Museo Goldoni

R. di S. Tomà

S. Angelo 1

S. Benedetto

R. di S. Luca

Rio di Ca' Michiel

Traghetto

S. Tomà 1, 82, N

Palazzo Corner Spinelli

Museo Fortuny

SANT'ORSOLA O TEATRO

Palazzo Balbi

Rio di Ca' Garzoni

R. di Ca' Sani

C. D. MANDOLA

Ca' Foscari

Palazzi Mocenigo

R. di S. Angelo

RIO TERRA ASSASSINI R. della Ve

C. VERONA

P. S. SAMUELE

CAMPO S. ANGELO

C. DE CAFFETTIER

C. NUOVO

Oratorio Annunziata

Palazzo Grassi

SAL S. SAMUELE

C. BOTTEGHE

C. D.
FENICE

Ca' Rezzonico

S. Samuele 3, 4, 82, N

CAMPO S. SAMUELE

SAL MALIPIERO

S. Stefano

La Fenice

Traghetto

S. Samuele

C. D. TEATRO

CAMPO SANTO STEFANO

R. d. Fenice

Ca' Rezzonico 1

CORTE STORZA

S. Maurizio

Ca' del Duca

R. del Duca

R. DEL TRAGHETTO

Palazzo Loredan

CAMPO S. MAURIZIO

S. Maria del Giglio

Palazzo Corner della Ca'Grande

R. Canal Zogia

R. di S. M. Zobenigo

CAMPO DEL TRAGHETTO

CAMPO PISANI

S. Vitale

R. S. Vidal

R. del Orso

Palazzo Pisani

R. di S. Stefano

Accademia 1, 3, 4, 82, N

PONTE D. ACCADEMIA

S. M. del Giglio 1

Traghetto

Accademia

CANAL GRANDE

Guggenheim Collection

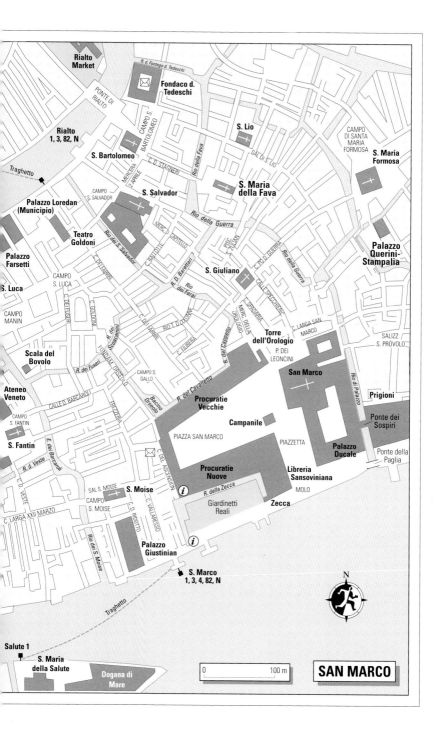

SAN MARCO

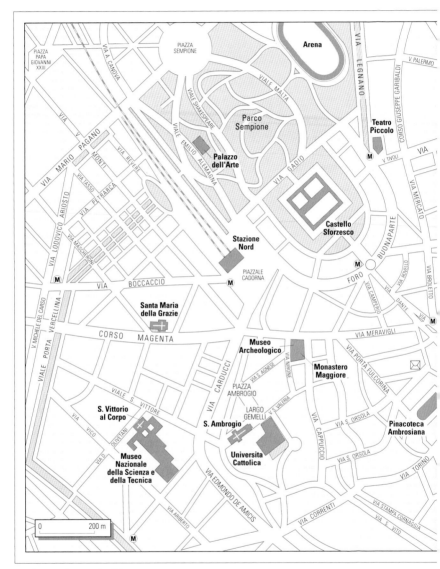

Map © Rough Guides Ltd, 1999

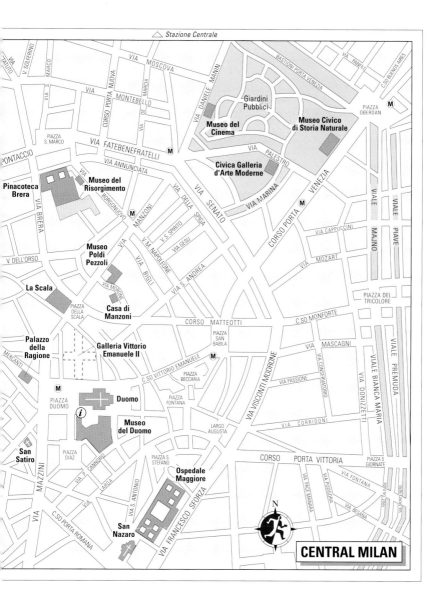

Stazione Centrale

CENTRAL MILAN

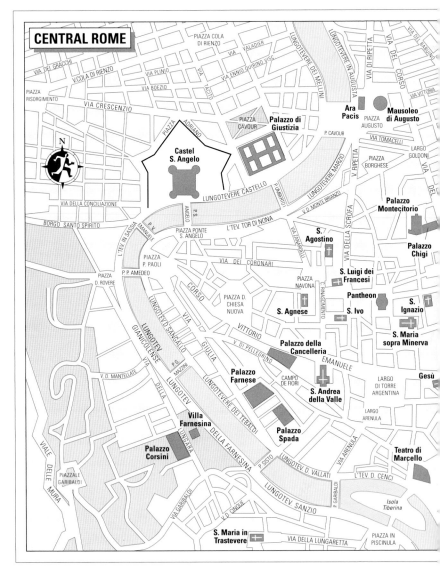

Map © Rough Guides Ltd, 1999

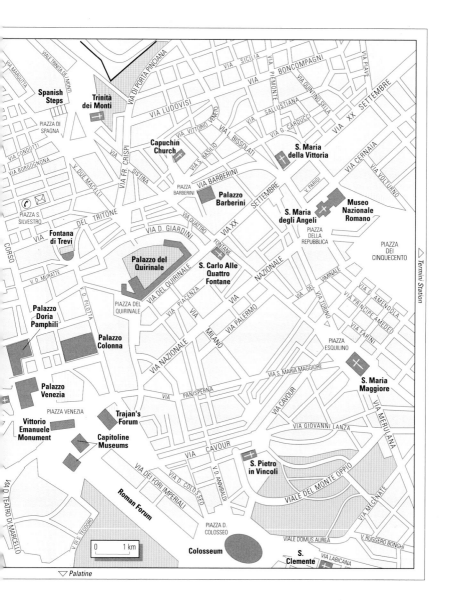

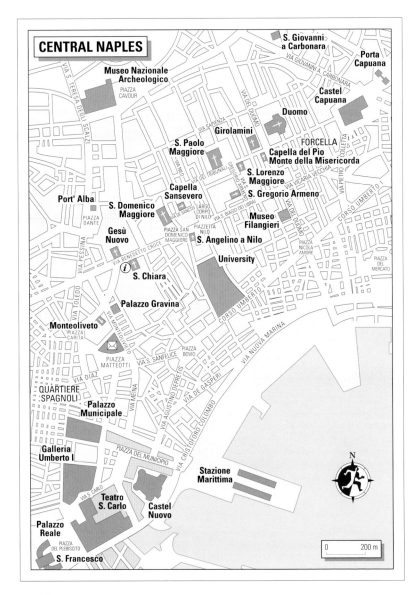

CENTRAL NAPLES

S. Giovanni a Carbonara
Porta Capuana
VIA GIOVANNI A CARBONARA
Museo Nazionale Archeologico
VIA S. TERESA DEGLI SCALZI
PIAZZA CAVOUR
Castel Capuana
VIA DEL DUOMO
VIA SAPIENZA
Duomo
Girolamini
S. Paolo Maggiore
FORCELLA
Capella del Pio Monte della Misericorda
VIA DEI TRIBUNALI
S. Lorenzo Maggiore
VIA VICARIA VECCHIA
VIA PIETRO COLLETTA
Capella Sansevero
S. Gregorio Armeno
Port' Alba
S. Domenico Maggiore
Museo Filangieri
CORSO UMBERTO
PIAZZA DANTE
VIA DE SANCTIS
LARGO CORPO DI NILO
VIA S. BIAGIO DEI LIBRAI
PIAZZA DEL MERCATO
Gesù Nuovo
PIAZZA SAN DOMENICO MAGGIORE
PIAZZETTA NILO
S. Angelino a Nilo
PIAZZA NICOLA AMORE
VIA PESSINA
VIA BENEDETTO CROCE
University
S. Chiara
Palazzo Gravina
CORSO UMBERTO
VIA TOLEDO
Monteoliveto
PIAZZA CARITÀ
VIA MONTEOLIVETO
PIAZZA BOVIO
VIA NUOVA MARINA
PIAZZA MATTEOTTI
VIA S. SANFELICE
VIA DIAZ
QUARTIERE SPAGNOLI
VIA MENA
VIA AGOSTINO DEPRETIS
VIA DE GASPERI
Palazzo Municipale
Galleria Umberto I
PIAZZA DEL MUNICIPIO
VIA CRISTOFORO COLOMBO
Stazione Marittima
N
VIA S. CARLO
Teatro S. Carlo
Castel Nuovo
Palazzo Reale
PIAZZA DEL PLEBISCITO
S. Francesco

0   200 m

Map © Rough Guides Ltd, 1999

VENICE (VENEZIA):

City estimated population 1998: 306,500.

Arthur Symons said of Venice 'A realist, in Venice would become a romantic, by mere faithfulness to what he saw before him.'

Venice is the capital of the provincia of Venezia and the regione of Veneto in northern Italy. It is one of the world's oldest and most popular tourist destinations and was the greatest seaport in Medieval Europe.

The city and its singularly strange location on the 118 islands of the Venetian Lagoon is criss-crossed by more than 150 canals and 400 bridges, and is divided into 6 districts: San Marco, Castello, Cannaregio, Santa Croce, San Polo and Dorsoduro. The settlement was established in the 5th and 6th centuries after barbarian invasions from the north pushed the inhabitants of the surrounding countryside onto the islands of the lagoon to save themselves. The most notable such invasions were Attilla the Hun's brutal invasion in 452 and Albion's Lombard invasion of 568.

In 466 a council of 12 townships was elected to give the refugee settlements a semblance of order. By 697 the first Doge, Paolo Lucio Anafesto, was elected to rule over the lagoon townships. Pepin's Frankish Invasion in 810 made the inhabitants of the lagoon move the emerging city at Malamocco to the easily defended cluster of islands at Riva Alto where the modern city of Venice now stands.

The city grew as a significant trading port and soon eclipsed the Byzantine Empire in importance. The Crusades at the end of the 11th century allowed the Venetians to gain control of trade across the Mediterranean and establish a trading empire across the eastern Mediterranean. The doges claimed the title of Lord of One Quarter and One Eighth of the Entire Byzantine Empire. This empire stretched across the Aegean islands, Peleponesia, Crete and part of Constantinople and the Venetians controlled many coastal forts on the Greek mainland.

The expansion of Venetian trade and the aggressive tactics displayed by Venetian traders encroached upon the trade of the Byzantine Empire and the emperor encouraged traders from Pisa and Genoa to compete for Byzantine trade. During the ensuing centuries Venice fought with Byzantium and vied with Genoa for maritime supremacy. In 1380 the Venetians defeated the Genoans and with naval supremacy assured they turned their attention towards the land. They captured and colonized Veneto and much of Lombardia and Emilia-Romagna.

The Turkish expansion into Europe in the 15th century did much to harm Venice's ports of trade and Venice embarked upon its long decline. Within a century the Venetian Republic had lost all its ports throughout the Mediterranean.

In 1797 Napoleon handed Venice to the Austrians for it to become part of the Austro-Hungarian Empire but reincorporated it into his Italian Kingdom in 1805. After his defeat Venice reverted once more to the Austrians and was not reunited with Italy until 1866.

TRANSPORT

Airport
Aeroporto di Venezia Marco Polo is 10 km from Venice and 25 km from Treviso.

Tel: (0)41 260-9260.

Trains
Stazione Santa Lucia is located alongside the Canal Grande in Cannaregio. The station is directly linked with Padova, Verona, Trieste and Bologna.

Train information Tel: (0)41 147888088.

Venice Simplon-Orient Express travels across Europe to and from major city destinations such as

London – Paris – Venice

Venice – Florence – Rome

Venice – Prague – Paris – London

Venice – Lucerne – Paris – London.

Tel: 0800 780-711.

Roads

The A4 from west or east, A13 to Padova, then A4 from south or A27 from north.

Your car may be left in the large car park on Tronchetto island.

The vaporetto line 3 or 4 or ferryboat line 17 will transport you to the island city.

Buses

ACTV buses alight at Piazzale Roma.

Local Transport

Vaporetti are Venice's answer to buses. Vaporetto 1 makes the journey from Piazzale Roma, up the Canal Grande to San Marco and then on to the Lido. A ride down the Grand Canal or the Giudecca Canal to Lido costs 4,000 lire (one way) and 7,200 lire (round-trip ticket), but you can buy a daily ticket for 15,000 lire, a three day ticket for 30,000 lire or a weekly ticket for 55,000 lire.

For Vaporetto timetables Tel: (0)41 238-1520.

Water Taxis are expensive but plentiful.

Gondolas are intrinsically and romantically linked with travel around Venice, but they are expensive.

Bacino Orseolo landing place for gondolas. Tel: (0)41 528-9316.

Calle Vallaresso landing place for gondolas. Tel: (0)41 520-5275.

TRAVELLERS INFORMATION

Tourist Offices

The Azienda di Promozione Turistica (APT) is in the Palazzetto Selva near Piazza San Marco.
Tel: (0)41 522-6356. Fax: (0)41 529-8730.

APT Head Office
Castello 4421, 30122 Venezia.
Tel: (0)41 529-8711. Fax: (0)41 523-0399.

Financial and Currency

The American Express Office is located at Salizzada San Moisè.
Tel: (0)41 520-0844.

The Thomas Cook Italia Office is at
San Marco 5126, 30100 Venezia.
Piazza San Marco.
Tel: (0)41 528-7358.

Post Office

The main Post Office is situated at:–
Piazzale Favretti, 30171 Venezia Mestre P.
Tel: (0)41 926-337.

Emergency

Public Emergencies and Assistance. Tel: 113.
Fire. Tel: 115.
Ambulance and Emergency Medical Assistance. Tel: 118.
Police. Tel: (0)41 274-8203 or 522-2612.

Consulate

UK: Dorsoduro 1051, 30100 Venezia.
Tel: (0)41 522-7207.

Landmarks

Piazza San Marco was described by Alfred de Musset as 'the drawing room of the world'. It has been the focal point of Venetian administration for over a millennium.

Basilica di San Marco, which dominates the eastern side of the Piazza San Marco, is the cathedral church of the city. This beautiful building is the third to stand on this location. It was commissioned by Doge Domenico Contarini in the 11th century. The original basilica dates back to the 9th century.

The **Palazzo Ducale** was the residence of the Doges until the fall of the Venetian Republic in 1797. This venetian-gothic palace houses master paintings by artists such as Tintoretto and Paolo Veronese.
   Piazza San Marco 1, 31024 Venezia.
   Tel: (0)41 522-4951.

The **Bell Tower of St. Mark** is known as 'El paron de casa' (the lord of the house). On 14 July 1902 it collapsed and had to be rebuilt, brick by brick. This massive structure dominates the square and the surrounding area.

The **Bridge of Sighs,** which spans the Rio di Palazzo, was built in about 1600 by Antonio Contino. It received its name during the 17th century. It is said that prisoners, crossing the bridge from the Palazzio Ducale on their way to the prison on the other side, would sigh at their last sight of the lagoon and the island of San Giorgio.

Sata Maria Gloriosa dei Frari is a huge gothic church that rises from San Polo. Titian's 'Assumption' hangs above the altar in the church wherein he is buried. Other works on show include the 'Madonna di Ca' Pesaro' and a statue of 'John the Baptist' by Donatello.

The baroque **Santa Maria della Salute** stands guard over the spot
where the Canal Grande opens into the San Marco Basin. It was
begun in the 1631 by Baldassare Longhena in honour of the Virgin
Mary, who, it was believed, saved the city from the plague. The main
part of the church is an octagon surmounted by a large dome. The
Festa della Salute takes place every year on 21 Nov. City workers lay
a pontoon bridge over the Grand Canal from the San Marco district to
the church. Venetians parade to pay tribute to the continued health of
the city and the Virgin Mary. Gondoliers visit to have their oars
blessed.

Museums and Galleries

Gallerie dell'Accademia is the biggest Venetian museum and is open
every day from 9.00 a.m. to 2.00 p.m. and from Tuesday to Thursday
9.00 a.m. to 7.00 p.m. The Gallerie is housed in the former church of
Santa Maria della Carità. The collection contains works from such
irrefutable masters as Giovanni Bellini, Tintoretto, Paolo Veneziano,
Titian and Paulo Veronese.
  Tel: (0)41 522-2247.

The **Peggy Guggenheim Collection** was bequeathed to the city in 1979
when Peggy Guggenheim died. It is located in San Gregorio. This
extensive collection of modern masters includes works by Picasso,
Kandinsky, Ernst, Chagall, Klee, Mirò and Dali, to name but a few.
  Tel: (0)41 520-6288.

The **Correr Museum** is housed in the Palazzo Pesaro, designed by
Baldassare Longhena. It is situated on the west side of the Piazza
San Marco and was begun with a donation to the city of Venice in
1830 by Teodoro Correr. This civic museum houses many Venetian
treasures.
  Tel: (0)41 522-5625.

Libreria Sansoviniani is located at the west side of the Piazzetta di San Marco. It was designed by Jacopo Sansovino and built in the 16th century. Inside the Libreria Sansoviniani are the **Libreria Marciana** and the **Museo Archelogico**.

FLORENCE (FIRENZE):

City est. population 1996: 380,000.

Founded in 59 BC as Florentia (The Flourishing Town), Florence had become a provincial capital and commercial centre of the Roman Empire by the 3rd century AD. Following the decline of the Empire, there were centuries of occupation, by the Ostrogoths then the Byzantines and ultimately the Lombards. Yet by the 10th century, under the guidance of Matilda of Tuscany, Florence once again prospered and was recognized as Tuscany's premier city.

In 1293 a constitution was adopted that forbade members of the nobility and labourers from holding power, facilitating the birth of a civil servant class vying for position in the Signoria (the government body). Members were elected for only two months leading to a climate of intrigue, alliances, inconstancy and political interest amongst the population; factors that would dictate Florentine politics in years to come.

Throughout the 12th and 13th centuries the economy grew and the dispute between the Guelfs (Papal supporters) and the Ghibelines (Imperial supporters) that had threatened stability ended in victory for a group of Guelf merchant families. In addition, Pisa, Siena, Pistoia and Arezzo all came into the city's sphere of influence during this time. Power was held principally by 7 guilds and political parties campaigned on broadly one of two issues – aggressive expansion, supported by the Neri (the rich merchants); and preservation of peace, voiced by the Bianchi, the lesser citizens. By the time of the Black Death in 1348 there was a population of 90,000, making it one of Europe's great cities. The plague, however, cut this figure in half and this combined with famine, a downturn in economic fortune and ultimately rebellion eroded Florence's power and splendour.

Ironically, it was this period of trouble that paved the way for the decline of the guilds and the emergence of merchants and bankers in civic life who would lead Florence through its greatest era, the Renaissance. Chief among these men of the 15th century were Giovanni Rucellai and Cosimo de' Medici. Medici particularly, who dominated Florentine life without ever holding official office, patronized all the arts and financed the building of the Medici Palace, the church of San Lorenzo and the Monastery of St. Mark. Artists of the calibre of Donatello, Boccaccio, Ghiberti and Michelangelo, among many others, were all active in the city. Cosimo's work was continued by his son, Piero, and his grandson, Lorenzo. On Lorenzo's death in 1494, Charles VII of France invaded with the support of the Florentine popular party, and a republic was declared. This brief interlude signalled the end of Florence's greatness.

In 1512 the Medicis returned in triumph only for another republic to be declared in 1527. It was overthrown in 1530 and in 1537 Cosimo de' Medici was made Duke of Florence by Emperor Charles V. He and his wife, Eleonora of Toledo, undertook the building of the Ufizzi, the renovation of the Palazzo Vecchio and the reconstruction of the Pitti Palace. Yet despite these achievements, there were to follow centuries of cultural and political anonymity. Florence had become a backwater of European power. The Medici dynasty ended with the death of Gian Gastone in 1737. Power went first to the Grand Duke of Tuscany, then Napoleon briefly and finally Leopold II of Hapsburg, who abdicated in favour of Italian King Vittorio Emanuele. In 1860, the city annexed itself to Italy and served as capital from 1865–70.

Following the reunification there was a time of ill-conceived restructuring and renovation, with both city population and boundaries growing haphazardly throughout the early 20th century. Further disastrous damage was to result from World War II and then a huge flood in 1966. It was this latter tragedy that was to expose the huge amount of work required to modernise the city and protect its treasures. It is a process that continues today with teams of dedicated experts working in often difficult and under-financed circumstances.

TRANSPORT

Airports
Aeroporto Amerigo Vespucci is a 15-minute train ride from the main station. The no. 62 bus also runs to and from the airport approximately every 20 minutes.

In addition, there are train services to Aeroporto Galileo Galilei at Pisa.

Trains
Stazione Santa Maria Novella is on Piazza Santa Maria Novella, opposite the church. It runs direct lines to Bologna, Milan, Rome and Venice.

Tel: (0)55 278785.

Roads
The A1 connects with Bologna and Milan in the north and Rome and Naples in the south. The A11 (Autostrada del Mare) connects with Prato, Lucca, Pisa and the coast, with a superstrada going to Siena. The S67 runs to Pisa in the west and Forlì and Ravenna in the east.

Buses

The main bus station is alongside Santa Maria Novella.

Local Transport

ATAF buses service the city centre. Tickets, which are available through tobacconists, vending machines and at larger bus stops, should be validated in the machines on the buses. It costs 1,500 lire for an hour-long ticket, 2,000 lire for 2 hours and 6,500 lire for 24 hours.

Taxis

Taxis operate 24 hours a day and may be hailed, found at taxi stands (main one at the railway station) or telephoned.

Tel: (0)55 4390 or (0)55 4798 or (0)55 4242.

TRAVELLERS INFORMATION

Tourist Office

Consorzio ITA is located at platform 16 in the main railway station and includes an accommodation service.

Tel: (0)55 282893 or (0)55 219537.

Financial and Currency

The American Express Office is on Via Dante Alighieri 20–22r.

Tel: (0)55 50981.

The Thomas Cook office is on Ponte Vecchio, Lungarno Acciaiuoli 6r.

Tel: (0)55 289781.

Currency exchange and cash withdrawals at banks and ATMs throughout the city.

Post Office

The main post office is on Via Pellicceria off Piazza della Repubblica.
Tel: (0)55 216122.

Emergency Numbers

Public Emergencies and Assistance. Tel: 113.

Fire. Tel: 115.

Ambulance and Emergency Medical Assistance. Tel: 118.

Police. Tel: 112.

Questura (to report tourist crime). Tel: (0)55 49771 (Via Zara 2).
Also an office on Piazza del Duomo.

24 hour Pharmacy. Farmacia Comunale by platform 16 at the train
station. Tel: (0)55 289435.

Consulates

U.K. Lungarno Corsini 2. Tel: (0)55 284133.

U.S. Lungarno Vespucci 38. Tel: (0)55 239-8276.

(For embassies, see under Diplomatic Representation on page 184.)

Internet Access

Internet Train. Via dell'Orvio 25r. Tel: (0)55 234-5322.

e-mail: info@infoline.it

6,000 lire for 30 minutes or 10,000 lire for an hour.

Landmarks

Piazza del Duomo

The red-brick duomo, created by Filippo Brunelleschi and the third
largest dome in the world, rises majestically over Florence. Opposite
is the Baptistry, decorated inside with Byzantine-style mosaics of
Dante's *Inferno*. Outside are Ghiberti's awe-inspiring 'Gates of
Paradise'. For unrivalled views of the city, climb the Campanile
(bell tower).

Palazzo Vecchio and Piazza della Signoria

Palazzo Vecchio, designed in the 13th century, is Florence's civic centre. The near-by Piazza della Signoria, massive and also designed in the 13th century, was the civic centre for a period. Here Savonarola denied the world some of the Renaissance's best art when he burnt it in the 'Bonfire of the Vanities'. He met a similar end in the same spot 12 months later. The square also incorporates the Loggia dei Lanzi, a gallery housing sculpture by the likes of Benvenuto Cellini and Giambologna.

Piazza Santa Croce

The Franciscan Chiesa di Santa Croce, regarded by many as the city's most beautiful church, is to be found in this square.

Ponte Vecchio

This world-famous bridge is also the oldest in Florence. The butchers and tanners of the 1500s have given way to jewellers, tourist shops and street performers. Lit up at night, there are still few more romantic settings.

Basilica di San Lorenzo and the Palazzo Medici

The interior was designed by Michelangelo, who, disillusioned with city politics, left for Rome halfway through the job. Still the buildings are magnificent and act as fitting testament, as they had hoped they would, to the Medici dynasty.

Palazzo Pitti

15th century palace that now houses 6 museums, including fine collections of Titian and Rubens. The wonderful gardens, Giardino di Boboli, provide the setting.

Piazzale Michelangelo

On top of a hill overlooking the city, there is a wonderful panoramic view to be had, especially at sunset.

Museums and Galleries

Galeria Uffizi

Off Palazzo Vecchio. One of the world's most famous art collections, it houses incomparable examples of the works of Botticelli, da Vinci, Michelangelo, Raphael, Titian, Giotto, Caravaggio, Cimabue, Rubens and Rembrandt. There are also fine Greek and Roman statuary. Some rooms are still closed following the terrorist bomb of 1993.

Tel: (0)55 471960.

Museo dell'Opera di Santa Maria del Fiore

Piazza del Duomo. Home to the Duomo's most important pieces, including a late Michelangelo *Pieta*.

Bargello

Piazza San Firenze. Previously a fortress, mansion and prison, now home to the Museo Nazionale including fine examples by Donatello and Michelangelo.

Galleria del Accademia

Via Ricasoli 60. Housing impressive collections of painting and sculpture, the undoubted highlight is Michelangelo's bravura *David*, completed when he was just 29. His unfinished *Slaves* are also here.

SOCIAL STATISTICS

Vital statistics (and rates per 1,000 population), 1997: Births, 528,901 (9·2); deaths, 533,078 (9·6); marriages, 273,111 (4·7); natural increase, −24,177 (−0·4); infant deaths, (up to 1 year of age) 3,436 (6·5 per 1,000 live births). Expectation of life: females, 81·3 years; males, 74·9.

Fertility rate, 1990–95, 1·2 births per woman.

In 1997 there were 3,459 suicides; 75·6% were men.

In 1997 there were 1m. legal immigrants living in Italy, plus an estimated 250,000 illegal immigrants. In 1995, 96,710 people emigrated from Italy and there were 99,105 immigrants into the country in 1994.

CLIMATE

The climate varies considerably with latitude. In the south, it is warm temperate, with little rain in the summer months, but the north is cool temperate with rainfall more evenly distributed over the year. Florence, Jan. 46·8°F (8·2°C), July 74·3°F (23·5°C). Annual rainfall 38" (974 mm). Milan, Jan. 37·9°F (3·3°C), July 68·3°F (20·2°C). Annual rainfall 32" (819 mm). Naples, Jan. 52·5°F (11·4°C), July 76·1°F (24·5°C). Annual rainfall 45" (1,143 mm). Palermo, Jan. 56·8°F (13·8°C), July 78·2°F (25·7°C). Annual rainfall 35" (897 mm). Rome, Jan. 48·4°F (9·1°C), July 74·3°F (23·5°C). Annual rainfall 30" (751 mm). Venice, Jan. 41·2°F (5·1°C), July 72·0°F (22·2°C). Annual rainfall 36" (926 mm).

CONSTITUTION AND GOVERNMENT

The Constitution dates from 1948. Italy is 'a democratic republic founded on work'. Parliament consists of the *Chamber of Deputies* and the *Senate*. The Chamber is elected for 5 years by universal and direct suffrage and consists of 630 deputies. The Senate is elected for 5 years on a regional basis by electors over the age of 25, with each region having at least 7 senators. There are 315 elected senators in all. The Valle d'Aosta is represented by 1 senator only, the Molise by 2. The President of the Republic can nominate 11 senators for life from eminent persons in the social, scientific, artistic and literary spheres. The President may become a senator for life. The *President* is elected in a joint session of Chamber and Senate, to which are added 3 delegates from each Regional Council (1 from the Valle d'Aosta). A two-thirds majority is required for the election, but after a third indecisive scrutiny the absolute majority of votes is sufficient. The President must be 50 years or over; term of office, 7 years. The Speaker of the Senate acts as the deputy President. The President can dissolve the chambers of parliament, except during the last 6 months of the presidential term. An attempt to create a new constitution, which had been under consideration for 18 months, collapsed in June 1998.

A *Constitutional Court*, consisting of 15 judges who are appointed, 5 each by the President, Parliament (in joint session) and the highest law and administrative courts, can decide on the constitutionality of laws and decrees, define the powers of the State and Regions, judge conflicts between the State and Regions and between Regions, and try the President and Ministers.

The revival of the Fascist Party is forbidden. Direct male descendants of King Victor Emmanuel are excluded from all public offices, have no right to vote or to be elected, and are banned from Italian territory; their estates are forfeit to the State. Titles of nobility are no longer recognized, but those existing before 28 Oct. 1922 are retained as part of the name.

A referendum was held in June 1991 to decide whether the system of preferential voting by indicating 4 candidates by their listed number should be changed to a simpler system, less open to abuse, of indicating a single candidate by name. The electorate was 46m. Turn-out was 62·5% (there was a 50% quorum). 95·6% of votes cast were in favour of the change. As a result, an electoral reform of 1993 provides for the replacement of proportional representation by a system in which 475 seats in the Chamber of Deputies are elected by a first-past-the-post single-round vote and 155 seats by proportional representation in a separate single-round vote on the same day. There are 27 electoral regions. There is a 4% threshold for entry to the Chamber of Deputies.

At a further referendum in April 1993, turn-out was 77%. Voters favoured the 8 reforms proposed, including a new system of election to the Senate and the abolition of some ministries. 75% of the Senate is now elected by a first-past-the-post system, the remainder by proportional representation; no party may present more than 1 candidate in each constituency. In July 1997 an all-party parliamentary commission on constitutional reform proposed a directly elected president with responsibility for defence and foreign policy, the devolving of powers to the regions, a reduction in the number of seats in the Senate and in the lower house and the creation of a third chamber to speak on behalf of the regions.

Reaction to the proposed reforms has been lukewarm. The original hope was that the 1948 constitution, which in the aftermath of Fascism had been designed to keep government weak, would be changed to give more power to the central administration. But this is only possible if a method of election is adopted that gives fewer opportunities to small parties to bring down coalitions on minor issues. The extent of the problem can be judged by the catalogue of post-war governments – 55 since 1947. The precarious nature of political authority in Italy is likely to remain while a quarter of parliamentary seats are elected by proportional representation on a party list basis.

But, for the moment, the argument is academic. Even the modest reforms proposed by the commission on parliamentary reform have been put on hold after apparently irreconcilable disagreements between the governing coalition of left democrats and the right wing opposition.

National Anthem

'Fratelli d'Italia' ('Brothers of Italy'; words by G. Mameli; tune by
M. Novaro, 1847).

RECENT ELECTIONS

Parliamentary elections were held on 21 April 1996. There were 1,574
candidates. The Olive Tree Alliance gained 284 seats in the Chamber
of Deputies and 157 in the Senate with 41·2% of the national vote, the
Freedom Alliance 246 and 116 with 37·3%, the Northern League 59
and 27 with 10·8%, the Refounded Communists 35 and 10 with 8·6%.
In the Chamber of Deputies minor parties won 6 seats. In the Senate
the Pannella List won 27 seats and minor parties won 4.

European Parliament. Italy has 87 representatives. At the June
1999 elections turn-out was 70·6%. Forza Italia gained 22 seats with
25·2% of votes cast (group in European Parliament: Group of the
European People's Party); the Party of the Democratic Left (former
Communists), 15 with 17·4% (European Socialist Party); the National
Alliance, 9 with 10·3% (Group Union for Europe). Other parties gained
7 seats or fewer.

CURRENT ADMINISTRATION

President: Carlo Azeglio Ciampi, b. 1920 (elected on 13 May 1999;
sworn in on 18 May).

The government in Sept. 1999 comprised (PDS = Democratic
Party of the Left; PPI = Popular Party; RI = Italian Renewal):

Prime Minister: Massimo D'Alema, b. 1949 (Democrats of the
Left/DS; sworn in 21 Oct. 1998).

Deputy Prime Minister: Sergio Mattarella (PPI). *Foreign Affairs:* Lamberto Dini (RI). *Finance:* Vincenzo Visco (PDS). *Interior:* Rosa Russo Jervolino (PPI). *Agriculture:* Paulo de Castro (Ind). *Education:* Luigi Berlinguer (PDS). *Environment:* Edo Ronchi (Greens). *Foreign Trade:* Piero Fassino (PDS). *Health:* Rosaria Bindi (PPI). *Industry:* Pierluigi Bersani (PDS). *Justice:* Oliviero Diliberto (PCDI). *Labour and Southern Affairs:* Cesare Salvi (PDS). *Communications:* Salvatore Cardinale (UDR). *Public Works:* Enrico Micheli (Ind). *Transport:* Tiziano Treu (RI). *Family and Social Affairs:* Livia Turco (PDS). *Equal Opportunities:* Laura Balbo (Greens). *Regional Affairs:* Katia Bellillo (PCDI). *Public Administration:* Angelo Piazza (SDI). *University and Scientific Research:* Ortensio Zecchino (PPI). *European Union Affairs:* Enrico Letta (PPI). *Relations with Parliament:* Gian Guido Folloni (UDR). *Culture:* Giovanna Mallandri (PDS). *Defence:* Carlo Scognamiglio (UDR). *Institutional Reforms:* Antonio Maccanico (PPI).

The *Speaker* is Luciano Voilante (PDS). The *Speaker of the Senate* is Nicola Mancini (PPI).

POLITICAL PROFILES

President of the Republic

Carlo Azeglio Ciampi

Carlo Ciampi was born in Livorno in 1920 and went to school and University in Pisa. Between 1941 and 1944 he served in the Italian army and was awarded the Military Cross. After World War II, he joined the Bank of Italy and between 1946 and 1960 he worked in various branches of the bank, carrying out administrative duties and inspections of commercial banks. He was made Secretary General in 1973, Deputy Director General in 1976 and Director General and Deputy Chairman of Ufficio Italiano dei Cambi in 1978. From 1979 to

1993 Ciampi served as Governor of the Bank of Italy and Chairman of the Ufficio Italiano dei Cambi. During this period he also served as Governor for Italy in the International Bank for Reconstruction and Development and similar international financial organizations, he was a member of the Group of Ten, and a member of the Board of Directors of the Cosiglio Nazionale delle Ricerche. From 1993 to 1994 Ciampi was Prime Minister, from 1994 to 1996 he was Vice President of the Bank for International Settlements and from 1995–96 he was Chairman of the EU Competitiveness Advisory Group and President of Instituto per l'Enciolopedia Treccani.

In 1996 Ciampi became Treasury Minister and he was elected President in May 1999.

Prime Minister

Massimo D'Alema

Massimo D'Alema was born in Rome on 20 April 1949. He completed his principal education at the University of Pisa where he studied philosophy. In 1963 he joined the FGCI (Youth Federation of Italian Communists) and then in 1968, the PCI (the Italian Communist Party). He became National Secretary of the FGCI in 1975 and joined the Central Committee of the PCI at the time of its XVth Congress. In 1983 D'Alema was made regional secretary of the PCI for Puglia and at the XVIIth Congress in 1986 he was reconfirmed both to the Central Committee and became part of the Secretariat. In 1987, he was elected for the first time to the Chamber of Deputies for the Brindisi-Taranto (Puglia) constituency. From 1988, together with Achille Occhetto, he was one of the leaders who transformed the PCI into the PDS and when the Democratic Party of the Left was born, he became its political co-ordinator. In the elections of 1992, he was re-elected for Brindisi-Taranto-Lecce and the same year he took up his duties as President of the PDS Deputies Group. In 1994 and again in 1996 he was re-elected, each time with increased votes. On 1 July 1994, he

was elected National Secretary of the Democratic Party of the Left
and on 5 Feb. 1997, President of the Parliamentary Commission for
Constitutional Reforms.

D'Alema is a professional journalist. His publications include:
Dialogo su Berlinguer (with Paul Ginsborg) (Conversations on
Berlinguer, Grunti, 1994); *Un Paese Normale, La Sinistra e il Futuro
dell'Italia* (An Ordinary Country, the Left and Italy's Future, Mondadori,
1995); *Progeuare il Futuro* (Planning the Future, Bompiani, 1995);
La Sinistra nell'Italia Cambia (The Party of the Left in a Changing Italy,
Feltrinelli, 1997); *La Grande Occasione* (The Great Opportunity,
Mondadori, 1997); and *l'Italia verso le Reforme* (Italy towards
Reform).

Minister for Foreign Affairs

Lamberto Dini

Lamberto Dini was born in Florence in 1931 and graduated from the
University of Florence in 1955. He went to the University of Minnesota
and Michigan from 1957 to 1959 where he completed his postgradu-
ate studies. He was the recipient of a Stringher Scholarship from the
Bank of Italy, a Fulbright Scholarship from the United States government and a fellowship from the Ford Foundation. From 1959 to 1975
Dini was an official of the International Monetary Fund and in 1976
was made Executive Director, a post he held until 1980. From 1979 to
1994, he was Director General of the Bank of Italy and a member of
the Monetary Committee of the European Economic Communities
from 1980 until 1994. Dini was elected Chairman of the deputies of the
group of Ten in 1981 and remained so until 1994. He was a member of
the Foundation Board of the International Centre for Monetary and
Banking Studies in Geneva from 1980 until 1995 (becoming president
in 1992). Lamberto Dini has been Governor for Italy on the
International Monetary Fund, the European Investment Bank, the
European Bank for Reconstruction and Development and the Inter

American Development Bank. He was President of the Council of Ministers and Minister of the Treasury from 1995 to 1996 and was Minister of Justice ad interim from Oct. 1995 to May 1996. Lamberto Dini was appointed Minister of Foreign Affairs on 18 May 1996.

Minister of Finance

Vincenzo Visco

Vincenzo Visco is a member of the Democratic Left Party and is one of their leading economists. He has already been Finance Minister once before when he served briefly in 1993 in Ciampi's cabinet, before resigning the day after taking office over a treasury decision not to authorize the corruption enquiries into ex-premier Bettino Craxi. Visco lectures at Pisa University and studied at UCLA Berkeley in the United States and at the University of York. He was first elected to parliament in 1983 where he was a member of the Lower House Finance and Treasury Committee for some years before being appointed Shadow Finance Minister by the then PDS leader, Achille Occhetto, in 1991. After the 1992 election he entered the Senate where he served as Deputy Secretary on the Finance and Treasury Committees. He was appointed Finance Minister in 1998.

Minister of Defence

Carlo Scognamiglio

Carlo Scognamiglio was born in 1945 and he graduated from Bocconi University in Milan with a degree in Economics. In the early 1970s, he did post-graduate studies at the London School of Economics. Scognamiglio has acted as technical consultant to a number of government ministers and he has been chairman of the Rizzoli-Corriere della Sera publishing group and deputy chairman of the former telecommunications monopoly, Stet. In 1992, Scognamiglio was elected Senator for the Italian Liberal Party in Milan. Two years later he was elected Senate Speaker. He was reconfirmed as Senator with the centre-right Freedom Front in 1994 and again in 1996, but he left Forza Italia in 1999 to become a founder member and second in command of the UDR. He was appointed Defence Minister in Oct. 1998.

President of the European Commission

Romano Prodi

Romano Prodi was born in 1939 in Bologna, where he attended school and University. He went on to study at the London School of Economics and Harvard Business School, establishing the considerable reputation as an economist that led to his appointment to the Chairmanship of the largest state owned company, IRI, where he served from 1982 to 1989. Romano Prodi's political career includes a term as Industry Minister from 1978 to 1979, and then, after severing his connections with the Christian Democrats, he founded the Olive Tree coalition – a centrist political group that drew on people from a broad cross-section of the political spectrum. In 1996, he formed Italy's 54th government since World War II with the overriding aim of taking Italy into the Euro. After the fall of the government in Oct. 1998, he decided to concentrate on his commitment to Europe. In 1999 he was elected as the President of the European Commission, taking up his post in Sept. 1999.

Silvio Berlusconi

Silvio Berlusconi is a rich and powerful media magnate and one-time Italian Prime Minister.

Born on 29 Sept. 1936 in Milan, Berlusconi graduated from the University of Milan and became an influential property developer. In 1974 he created Telemilano, a cable television business, and established the first commercial television network in Italy, Canale 5. There seemed no end to his voracious business appetite. He acquired department stores, publishing companies, media businesses and AC Milan football team, all under the umbrella of Fininvest Holding Company.

In 1994 Berlusconi found himself in the political arena. The parliamentary coalition, the Christian Democrats and Italian Socialist Party, had been decimated by corruption. Berlusconi established Forza Italia and announced that he was running for parliament. Having formed an alliance with the right-wing Northern League and the extreme right-wing National Alliance, his coalition party won the election with a 118-seat majority as the Freedom Alliance. Berlusconi was sworn in as Prime Minister on 11 May 1994.

Berlusconi's election campaign was fought on a free enterprise premise and he spoke against government intervention in private business. Despite the public's belief that Berlusconi would conduct an overhaul of the corrupt Italian political regime he took some time in forming his cabinet and it seemed that the old inactivity, borne of in-house squabbling, was still rife. Berlusconi then issued a decree against preventative detention. Overnight 1,859 prisoners, some suspected of drug trafficking, car theft and corruption, walked free from jail. A confrontation between Berlusconi and a group of well-respected Milanese magistrates, known as the Milan Pool, was inevitable. The Milan Pool went live on television and threatened to resign. Berlusconi conceded. Rumours were circulating that despite Berlusconi's claims that the decree was intended to resist Italy's decline into a 'police state', the real intention was to circumvent investigations of corruption into the Fininvest Holding Company and to protect his brother and business partner, Paolo.

Paolo Berlusconi later received a five months suspended sentence and confessed that he had established a 'slush fund' of almost $2m. to safeguard Fininvest Holding Company by bribing the State Finance Police. Silvio Berlusconi then became concerned that he might be the next to be investigated.

Berlusconi's parliament produced a budget that cut welfare spending and pensions. This inspired the three principal trade unions to begin strike action. After allegations of 'conflict of interest' magistrates questioned Berlusconi about his business practices. On 22 Dec. 1994 Berlusconi resigned from his post and became merely a caretaker Prime Minister of Italy after a vote of no confidence.

LOCAL GOVERNMENT

Italy is administratively divided into 15 autonomous regions and 5 autonomous regions with a special constitutional status; these are subdivided into 102 provinces and 1,230 municipalities. The regions have their own councils and governments with certain legislative and administrative functions adapted to the circumstances of each region. A government commissioner co-ordinates regional and national activities. Since 1993 mayors have been directly elected for 4-year terms in towns of more than 15,000 inhabitants and allot 60% of seats on municipal councils, the remainder being apportioned according to party vote.

Measures for the autonomy of the largely German-speaking **Alto Adige** (South Tyrol) were granted in Jan. 1992 and accepted by Austria in June 1992.

A powerful separatist movement, the Northern League, campaigns for autonomy for the regions around the Po Valley. Local government elections were held on 27 April 1997 and 11 May 1997, involving 11 provinces and 1,192 communes. The electorate was 14·4m. Regional elections held in Nov. 1997 resulted in landslide victories for the ruling centre-left coalition. In mayoral elections on 7 June 1998 the ruling centre-left coalition gained only 5 out of 16 seats in provincial capitals, with the centre-right Freedom Alliance winning 10 seats. The centrist former Christian Democrats took one seat.

DEFENCE

Budget

Defence expenditure, in lira:

1995 expenditure	31,561,000m. (US$19,375m.)
1996 expenditure	36,170,000m. (US$22,892m.)
1997 expenditure	37,190,000m. (US$24,260m.)
1998 budget	31,000,000m. (US$17,485m.)
1999 budget	30,854,000m. (US$18,711m.)

In the 1999 budget, 4,630,000m. lira (15%) is allocated for procurement. Acquisition of Eurofighter for the Air Force is being part-financed by loans. The defence budget includes expenditure for the Carabinieri, as part of the Army.

Strength of Armed Forces

The active strength of the Armed Forces is:

Central Staff	29,200	
Army	165,600	
Navy	40,000	(includes Naval Air and Marines)
Air Force	63,600	
Total	*298,400*	

The strength of the Armed Forces is being reduced and is planned to be 215,000 by 2005. The total strength of the Reserves available for immediate mobilization is about 304,000 (Army, 240,000; Navy, 36,000; Air Force, 28,000).

Paramilitary Forces

The Carabinieri, currently part of the Army, has a strength of 113,200. Proposals going through Parliament envisage control of the Carabinieri passing from the Ministry of Defence to the Ministry of the Interior when the Corps is deployed for public order. The Ministry of the Interior controls some 79,000 Public Security Guards. The Treasury Department contains about 63,500 Finance Guards.

Conscription

Conscription is for 10 months, with the conversion to fully professional Armed Forces planned to be completed by 2005. Of the Armed Forces' strength of 298,400, about 135,00 (45%) are conscripts. Within the Services, approximately 60% of the Army, 40% of the Navy and 35% of the Air Force are conscripts. Abolition of conscription is opposed by the Roman Catholic Church, whose charitable activities rely heavily on young men who opt for 'social service' as an alternative to the Services.

Nuclear Capability

Italy has no nuclear weapons.

Policy

The Kosovo Campaign, largely conducted from NATO bases on Italian territory, witnessed a significant change in Italian foreign policy. Support for the Campaign was remarkable in that Italy's two main political trends, Communism and Christian democracy, had led to a marked pacifist strain. Two distinct strands of opinion remain in Italian foreign policy. On the one hand is the traditional mediator role, involving basic support for the United States and the European Union allied with strong links with countries on the periphery of the international community. The second strand recommends a move away from the mediator role and suggests unqualified support for both NATO and the European Union. The Italian and United Kingdom Prime Ministers issued a joint declaration on 20 July 1999 that 'among the other lessons of [the] Kosovo' Campaign was 'a pressing need for improved European military capabilities'.

In 1999, before the Kosovo Campaign, 5 missions had been identified for the definition of the future structure of the Armed Forces:

a) Defending national territory, maritime and air spaces as well as lines of communication.

b) Participating in NATO collective defence.

c) Participating in multi-national operations in support of collective peace and security.

d) Contributing to the safeguarding of free institutions.

e) Participating in national disaster-relief activities.

The above objectives call for a greater capability with a reduced number of personnel and for the Services to be configured jointly for operational service. Plans include an increased capacity to project air power. The aircraft carrier *Giuseppe Garibaldi* is to be complemented by a new multi-role carrier which is expected to be operational in 2006.

INTERNATIONAL RELATIONS

Italy is a member of the UN, NATO, EU, WEU and the Central European Initiative. Italy is a signatory to the Schengen Accord of June 1990 which abolishes border controls between Italy and Austria, Belgium, Denmark, Finland, France, Germany, Greece, Iceland, Luxembourg, the Netherlands, Norway, Portugal, Spain and Sweden.

ECONOMY

Despite weak government, the Italian economy has made impressive advances in recent years. Inflation had come down from 5·6% in 1992 to 1·4% in 1997, the lira has stabilized and the balance of payments, in deficit at the beginning of the decade, is now comfortably in surplus. As a result Italy qualified for membership of the single European currency, an achievement few would have predicted in 1992 when the lira was forced out of Europe's exchange rate mechanism.

Italy's GNP per capita in 1996 for purchasing power was $19,890.

Policy

The government is committed to a reduction in borrowing, a strong currency and low inflation. It has embarked on an ambitious privatization programme to reduce radically its presence in industry and banking. In 1997 the government completed its biggest privatization to date with the 26,000bn. lire flotation of Telecom Italia. It also sold a third tranche in the ENI oil and gas group, privatized the Banca di Roma, Italy's second largest banking group, and pursued this programme with further sell-offs in 1998, including the sale of a fourth tranche in ENI.

In May 1998 Italy became one of the 11 founder members of the EMU. The OECD reports that with this primary political objective achieved, the tasks of economic policy are to consolidate the progress made on the macroeconomic front, and implement the structural reforms needed for faster employment growth.

Further anticipated economic reforms include the deregulation of the retail sector (ending rules specifying the categories of product to be sold in each shop), structural changes to turn around Italy's loss-making railways and postal services and reductions in the tax burden which, in 1998, was close to 44% of GDP.

Performance

Total GDP was US$1,166bn. in 1998. Real GDP growth in 1998 was 1·4%, and forecast to be 1·3% in 1999, the lowest of any of the euro-11 economies. With the terms of trade improving and import growth decelerating, the trade surplus is expected to grow despite the adverse affects of currency depreciation in Asian countries. The OECD commented that this, together with the projected disappearance of the deficit on the invisible account, may keep the current account surplus close to 3·5% in 1999, reinforcing Italy's newly-achieved position as a net creditor *vis-à-vis* the rest of the world.

Budget

Total revenue and expenditure for fiscal years, in 1,000bn. lire:

	Revenue	Expenditure		Revenue	Expenditure
1991	456,995	579,966	1994	504,320	641,910
1992	512,718	627,579	1995	557,657	699,534
1993	516,655	663,237	1996	591,991	727,402

Budgets for 1998 (and 1997) in 1,000,000m. lire: revenue, 581,188 (591,161) of which tax 546,188 (554,194); expenditure, 673,182 (690,737) of which capital expenditure 68,598 (67,070) and interest payments 181,121 (193,002).

The 1998 budget provided for an increase in value-added tax. Some reforms due to take place in 1998 were meant to reallocate the existing tax burden in a more business-friendly way. The rate of corporation tax was to come down from 53·2% to 37%. Other measure include reducing social security contributions, and a new two-tier income tax, brought in to encourage entrepreneurs to reinvest in profits and issue equity. Accompanying the tax reform was the devolution of substantial taxing powers from the central government to the regions.

VAT is 20% (reduced rate, 10%).

The public debt at 31 Dec. 1997 totalled 2,100,686,000m. lire. Between 1992 and 1997 the public deficit came down from more than 10% to 3%, or possibly less, of gross domestic product. Interest rates have also declined significantly.

Currency

On 1 Jan. 1999 the euro (EUR) became the legal currency in Italy and the *lira* became a subdivision of it; irrevocable conversion rate 1,936·27 lira to 1 euro. The euro, which consists of 100 cents, will not be in circulation until 1 Jan. 2002. There will be 7 euro notes in different colours and sizes denominated in 500, 200, 100, 50, 20, 10 and 5 euros, and 8 coins denominated in 2 and 1 euros, then 50, 20, 10, 5, 2 and 1 cents. Even though notes and coins will not be introduced until 1 Jan. 2002 the euro can be used in banking; by means of cheques, travellers' cheques, bank transfers, credit cards and electronic purses. Banking will be possible in both euros and lire until the lira is withdrawn from circulation – which must be by 1 July 2002.

The *lira* (ITL) notionally consists of 100 *centesimi*. The Economic Bulletin reported that 'professional forecasters expect inflation to decline to just above 1% in line with the forecast for the euro area as a whole'. The lira left the ERM in Sept. 1993 and rejoined in Nov. 1996. Gold reserves were 66·67m. troy oz. in Feb. 1998 and foreign exchange reserves were US$51,542m. Total money supply in Dec. 1997 was 646,000bn. lire.

Banking and Finance

The bank of issue is the Bank of Italy (founded 1893). It is owned by public-sector banks. Its *governor* (Antonio Fazio, b. 1936) is selected without fixed term by the 13 directors of the Bank's non-executive board. In 1991 it received increased responsibility for the supervision of banking and stock exchange affairs, and in 1993 greater independence from the government. Its gold reserve amounted to 40,929bn. lire in Dec. 1998; the foreign credit reserves of the Exchange Bureau (*Ufficio Italiano Cambi*) amounted to 88,611bn. lire.

The number of banks has gradually been declining in recent years, from 1,156 in 1990 to 921 in 1998. Of the 921 banks in 1998, 562 were co-operative banks.

The 'Amato' law of July 1990 gave public sector banks the right to become joint stock companies and permitted the placing of up to 49% of their equity with private shareholders.

On 31 Dec. 1997 the post office savings banks had deposits and current accounts of 307,481,000m. lire. On 31 Dec. 1998 credit institutions had deposits of 892,091bn. lire.

Legislation reforming stock markets came into effect in Dec. 1990. In 1996 local stock exchanges, relics of pre-unification Italy, were closed, and stock exchange activities concentrated in Milan.

Central Bank

Banca d'Italia

Founded 1893. Has sole right to issue notes in Italy.

Via Nazionale 91, 00184 Roma. Tel: (0)6 47921 Fax: (0)6 4792-2983

Commercial Banks

Banca Agricola Milanese

Via Mazzini 9–11, 20123 Milano. Fax: (0)2 8693-745

Banca Commerciale Italiana

Piazza della Scala 6, 20121 Milano. Fax: (0)2 8850-2173

Banca Toscana SpA

Via del Corso 6, 50122 Firenze. Tel: 05543911 Fax: (0)55 4391-742

Banco di Roma SpA

Piazza T Edison 1, 20123 Milano. Tel: (0)2 72291 Fax: (0)2 7229-2471

Banco Ambrosiano Veneto – Relazione Esterne

Piazza Ferrari 10, 20100 Milano. Tel: (0)2 8550-2173
Fax: (0)2 7239-5137

Banca Commerciale Italiana

Piazza della Scala 6, 20121 Milano. Tel: (0)2 8850
Fax: (0)2 8850-2173

Financial Institutions

Centrobanca (Banca Centrale di Credito Populare) SpA:
Founded 1946. Central organization for operations of Banche
Populare (co-operative banks) throughout Italy.
Corso Europa 20, 20122 Milano. Tel: (0)2 77811 Fax: (0)2 784-372

Instituto di Credito delle Casse di Rispiarmo Italiane SpA (ICCRI): Founded 1919. Central organization for operations of Casse di Rispiarmo throughout Italy.

Via San Basilio 15, 00187 Roma. Tel: (0)6 47151 Fax: (0)6 4715-3579

Bankers Organizations

Associazione Bancaria Italiana:

Founded 1919. Membership comprised of banks and savings banks, associations of banks and financial intermediaries.

Piazza del Gesù 49, 00186 Roma. Tel: (0)6 67671 Fax: (0)6 6767-457

Via della Posta 3, 20123 Milano. Tel: (0)2 8645-0695

Fax: (0)2 878-684

Stock Exchange

Commissione Nazionale per le Società e la Boursa (CONSOB):

Founded 1974. The Commission for Companies and the Stock Exchange. Exercises regulatory control over companies quoted on the stock exchange, convertible bonds, unlisted securities, insider trading and all forms of public saving except bank deposits and mutual funds.

Via Isonzo 19, 00198 Roma. Tel: (0)6 84771

Italian Stock Exchange/Italian Derivatives Market

Piazza degli Affari 6, 20123 Milano. Tel: (0)2 7242-6202

Fax: (0)2 7200-4333

Regional Stock Exchanges

Genoa: Borsa Valori, Via G. Boccardo 1, Genoa. Tel: (0)10 2094-400

Naples: Borsa Valori, Palazzo Borsa, Piazza Bovio, Naples.

Tel: (0)81 269-151

Rome: Borsa Valori, Via dei Burro 147, 00186 Roma.

Tel: (0)6 6792-701

Turin: Borsa Valori, Via San Francesco da Paola 28, Torino.

Tel: (0)11 547-743 Fax: (0)11 5612-193

Insurance Association

Associazione Nazionale fra le Imprese Assicuratrici (ANIA):

Founded 1944. Has 216 members of insurance companies.

Piazza S. Babila 1, 20122 Milano. Tel: (0)2 77641 Fax: (0)2 780-870

Chambers of Commerce

There are Chambers of Commerce in all regional major towns and cities.

Unione delle Camere di Commercio, Industria, Artiginato e Agricoltura (Italian Union of Chambers of Commerce, Industry, Crafts and Agriculture):

Founded 1954 to promote the development of Chambers of Commerce.

Piazza Sallustio 21, 00187 Roma. Tel: (0)6 47041

Weights and Measures

The metric system is in use. 1 quintal = 100 kg.

ENERGY AND NATURAL RESOURCES

Electricity

Installed capacity was 57·19m. kW in 1994. In 1997 the total power generated was 251,462m. kWh, of which 46,676m. kWh were generated by hydro-electric plants. Consumption in 1997 was 253,673m. kWh, of which 58,507m. kWh was for domestic use. Consumption per capita was an estimated 4,238 kWh in 1995.

Oil and Gas

Oil production, 1997, 5,892,055 tonnes. In 1997, natural gas production in 1,000 cu. metres was 19,123,396.

Minerals

Fuel and mineral resources fail to meet needs. Only sulphur and mercury yield a substantial surplus for exports.

Production of metals and minerals (in tonnes) was as follows:

	1993	1994	1995	1996	1997
Cement	13,902,392	12,285,703	11,733,556	12,480,388	12,166,878
Bentonite	150,503	326,992	590,845	471,535	511,760
Zinc	62,558	7,379	43,669	20,137	15,416
Sulphur	3,503,891	3,021,427	3,430,374	3,528,120	. . .
Lead	27,475	8,011	22,658	20,260	17,630
Feldspar	1,387,968	1,534,421	2,199,315	2,287,086	2,118,117

Agriculture

In 1997, 1,872,000 persons were dependent on agriculture, of whom 1,370,000 were economically active. In 1993 there were 205,819 sq. km of agricultural and forest lands, distributed as follows (in 1,000 ha): Forage and pasture, 6,746; woods, 5,874; cereals, 4,214; olive trees, 1,106; vines, 899; garden produce, 597; leguminous plants, 97.

At the 1991 census agricultural holdings numbered 3,023,344 and covered 22,702,356 ha. 2,893,145 owners (95·7%) farmed directly 15,961,093 ha (70·3%); 118,020 owners (3·9%) worked with hired labour on 6,603,522 ha (29·1%); 95,045 share-croppers (3·1%) tilled 1,208,337 ha (5·3%); the remaining 12,179 holdings (0·4%) of 137,740 ha (0·6%) were operated in other ways. By 1997, agricultural and forest lands covered 20,445,268 ha, of which 14,753,107 ha was in active agricultural use. There were 2·5m. farms in 1998. Agriculture accounts for 2·7% of GDP, 7·1% of exports and 15·3% of imports.

In 1994, 1,470,000 tractors were in use.

The production of the principal crops (in 1,000 metric quintals) in 1997: Sugar beet, 135,794; maize, 99,926; wheat, 68,156; tomatoes, 55,340; potatoes, 20,088; oranges, 18,092; barley, 11,491; rice,

14,240; olives, 35,274; lemons, 6,062; tangerines, mandarins and clementines, 5,131; oats, 2,761; grapes for wine, 67,543; tobacco (in tonnes), 1,325 (1996).

Livestock, 1996: Cattle, 7,173,932; sheep, 1,094,245; pigs, 8,171,092; goats, 1,098,543; horses, 315 (1995); donkeys, 26 (1995); mules, 12 (1995); chickens for meat, 115,359,613; poultry farming, 191,549,016.

Livestock products, 1996 (in 1,000 quintals): Milk, 118,184; meat, 37,451; cheese, 9,845; wool, 117; eggs, 6,971 (1,000 pieces).

Forestry
In 1995 forests covered 6·77m. ha or 22·5% of the total land area. Timber production was 9·8m. cu. metres in 1995.

Fisheries
The fishing fleet comprised, in 1994, 15,798 motor boats of 245,637 gross tonnes. The catch in 1996 was 3,325,990 quintals, of which 3,258,346 quintals were from marine waters.

INDUSTRY

Industry accounted for 25·6% of GDP in 1997. The main branches of industry are (% of industrial value added at factor cost in 1996) Textiles, clothing, leather and footwear (11·2%), food, beverages and tobacco (8·0%), energy products (11·8%), agricultural and industrial machines (9·2%), metal products except machines and means of transport (8·9%), mineral and non-metallic mineral products (5·8%), timber and wooden furniture (4·5%), electric plants and equipment (6·7%), chemicals and pharmaceuticals (8·2%), means of transport (5·4%).

Production, 1997: Motor vehicles, 199,251; artificial and synthetic fibres (including staple fibre and waste), 690,494 tonnes; cement, 33,718,169 tonnes; polyethylene resins, 1,065,115 tonnes; steel, 24,284,985 tonnes (1996).

Top Ten Companies

Company	Industry	Revenue ($m.)	World Ranking
Fiat Group	Automobiles	52,590	20
ENI	Energy Sources	35,651	38
Generali Group	Insurance	26,759	65
Telecom Italia	Telecommunications	25,140	76
Montedison Group	Multi-Industry	13,903	161
Sanpaolo Bank	Banking	11,876	204
Banca Commerciale Italiana	Banking	9,925	249
Banca di Roma	Banking	9,379	256
Credito Italiano	Banking	9,126	266
Finmeccanica	Aerospace and military technology	8,973	269
Pirelli Group	Industrial components	6,615	370
Alitalia Group	Transportation and airlines	5,230	456
Parmalat Finanzaria	Food and household products	4,181	579

Labour

In 1997 the workforce was 22,892,000 (8,685,000 females) of whom 20,087,000 were employed. 2,805,000 (1,457,000 females) were unemployed and looking for work – a rate of 12·2% – although only 1,031,000 (424,000) were actually registered. In 1996, 60·9% of the workforce were in services, 32·1% in industry and 7% in agriculture. There are strong indications of labour markets having become less rigid, especially in the north. In the centre and north unemployment was 6·9% in July 1998; in the relatively poor south, it was 22·5%. In

1995 the difference in the unemployment rates in the north and in the south was 14%, compared to a difference of just 2% in the 1960s. Over 50% of Italy's jobless have been out of work for more than a year. Pensionable retirement age was 60 for men and 55 for women in 1991, but this is being progressively raised to 65 for both sexes. Agreements between the government, employers and trade unions in 1992 and 1993 ended automatic wage indexation and regulated labour relations and wage increases. There are plans to introduce a 35-hour week in 2001.

In 1997 parliament approved the so-called 'Trev Package', which involves a large number of institutional changes regarding working hours and apprenticeships, mainly for young people from the south, and the introduction of employment agencies.

Employers Association
Confederazione Generale dell'Industria Italiana – CONFINDUSTRIA (General Confederation of Italian Industry):

Founded 1919. Comprises 109,000 firms and 4·2m. employees. Offices throughout Italy and in Brussels.

Viale dell'Astronomia 30, EUR, 00144 Roma. Tel: (0)6 59031 Fax: (0)6 5903-684

Trade Unions
There are 3 main groups: the Confederazione Generale Italiana del Lavoro (CGIL; no longer Communist-dominated), the Confederazione Italiana Sindacati Lavoratori (CISL; Catholic), and the Unione Italiana del Lavoro (UIL). Membership in 1994: CGIL, 5·2m. (2·7m. retired); CISL, 3·7m. (1·5m. retired); UIL, 1·7m. (0·5m. retired). In referendums held in June 1995 the electorate voted to remove some restrictions on trade union representation, end government involvement in public sector trade unions and end the automatic deduction of trade union dues from wage packets.

The three main Trade Union Federations are closely linked with political parties. The CGIL was formerly dominated by the Partito Comunista Italiano (Italian Communist Party) now by the Partito Democratico della Sinistra (Democratic Party of the Left). The CISL has links with the Partito Populare Italiano (Italian Popular Party – formerly Christian Democratic Party) and the UIL is associated with the Socialists.

Confederazione Generale Italiana de Lavoro (CGIL)

Founded 1944. Federation of 17 unions with over 5m. members.
Corso d'Italia 25, 00198 Roma. Tel: (0)6 84761

Confederazione Italiana Sindicati Lavatori (CISL)

Founded 1950. Affiliated to the International Confederation of Free Trade Unions and the European Trade Union Confederation.
Via Po 21, 00198 Roma. Tel: (0)6 84731 Fax: (0)6 8413-782

Unione Italiana del Lavoro (UIL)

Founded 1950. Associated to the International Confederation of Free Trade Unions and the European Trade Union Confederation with 1·5m. members from 35 national trade unions and 95 provincial union councils.

INTERNATIONAL TRADE

Foreign debt in Dec. 1996 was 68,013bn. lire.

Imports and Exports

The territory covered by foreign trade statistics includes Italy and San Marino, but excludes the municipalities of Livigno and Campione.
The following table shows the value of Italy's foreign trade (in 1,000m. lire):

	1993	**1994**	**1995**	**1996**	**1997**
Imports	232,991	272,382	335,661	321,286	354,456
Exports	266,214	308,046	381,175	388,885	405,732

Percentage of trade with EU countries in 1998: Exports, 56·2%; imports, 61·3%. Principal export markets, 1998 (% of total trade): Germany, 16·5%; France, 12·7%; USA, 8·5%; UK, 7·2%. Principal import suppliers: Germany, 18·8%; France, 13·1%; UK, 6·4%; USA, 5·1%.

Exports/imports by category, 1997 (in 1,000m. lire):

	Exports	**Imports**
Metal products and machinery	145,295	84,249
Textiles and leather goods	67,157	26,992
Wood, paper and rubber goods	52,101	29,237
Transport equipment	39,863	42,974
Chemical products	34,946	49,872
Foodstuffs, beverages and tobacco	16,841	24,831
Metallic minerals	16,439	32,422
Non-metallic minerals and products	15,866	6,094
Agricultural, forestry and fish products	10,430	20,455
Energy	6,800	37,330

The OECD reports that Italy's competitiveness in some important export sectors was affected by the devaluations in 1998 in Asia, but export performance is sound and export-market growth remains quite buoyant.

Export Institute

Istituto Nazionale per il Commercio Estero (ICE) (National Institute for Foreign Trade);

Founded 1919. Government agency for the promotion of foreign trade.

Via Liszt 21, 00144 Roma. Tel: (0)6 59921 Fax: (0)6 5992-6889
Email ice@ice.it

Selected Trade Shows and Exhibitions

Trade Show	Month	Frequency	Location
Arte Fiera International Fair of Contemporary Art Tel: (0)51 282-111	Jan.	Annual	Bologna
Intemare Underwater Lingerie & Swimwear Tel: (0)2 4801-5026	Feb. & July	Twice annually	Milan
Saidue Interior Architecture Show Tel: (0)2 2901-7144	March	Annual	Milan
Children's Book Fair Tel: (0)51 282-111	April	Annual	Bologna
International Furniture Exhibition Tel: (0)2 725941	April	Annual	Milan
La Fiera Bologna International Trade Fair Tel: (0)51 282-111	June	Annual	Bologna
SAIE International Building Exhibition Tel: (0)51 282-111	Oct.	Annual	Bologna

National Exhibition of Sports	Oct.	Annual	Florence
Fishing Equipment		
Tel: (0)55 476-870		

| Motor Show | Dec. | Annual | Bologna |
| Tel: (0)51 6451-011 |||

For further trade shows and exhibitions visit the Website on: www.bolognafiere.it/calendario_main_gb.html

COMMUNICATIONS

Roads

Roads totalled 316,400 km in 1996, of which 9,500 km were motorway, 46,900 km were highways and main roads, 118,000 km were secondary roads and 142,000 km other roads. In 1996 there were 38,586,000 motor vehicles, made up of: Passenger cars, 32,789,000 (568 per 1,000 inhabitants); buses and coaches, 78,000; vans and trucks, 5,719,000. There were 6,512 fatalities in traffic accidents in 1995 (6,578 in 1994).

Direzione Generale dell Motorizzazione Civile e del Transporti in Concessione

Controls road transport and traffic and public transport services (railways operated by private companies, buses, trolley buses, funicular railways and inland waterways). Via Giuseppe Caraci 36, 00157 Rome. Tel: (0)6 41581 Fax: (0)6 4158-2211

Azienda Nazionale Autonoma delle Strade (ANAS) (National Autonomous Road Corp.)

Founded 1928. Responsible for the administration of state roads and their improvement and extension.

Via Monzambano 10, 00185 Roma. Tel: (0)6 44461

Rules of the Road

Driving in Italy is on the right side of the road. Unless otherwise indicated, priority is given to cars coming from the right. Seat belts are compulsory. Random breath tests are made throughout Italy, especially near nightspots and after road accidents. Speed limits (unless otherwise indicated) are:

Motorway: (Autostrada): 130 km/h 1,100cc and over, 110km/h under 1,100cc.

Main non-urban highways: 110 km/h.

Secondary non-urban highways: 90 km/h.

Built up areas: 40 km/h.

Helmets are compulsory on mopeds up to age 18 and on all motorcycles.

Rail

Total of railways (1995), 19,485 km. The state-run railway (*Ferrovie dello Stato*) was 15,955 km (10,202 km electrified). In 1997 the state railways carried 461,000,000 passengers and 82,744,000 tonnes of freight. There are metros in Milan (68 km) and Rome (33·5 km), and tram/light rail networks in Genoa (2·3 km), Milan (240 km), Naples (23 km), Trieste and Turin (119 km).

Ferrovie dello Stato, SpA

Piazza della Croice Rossa 1, 00161 Roma. Tel: (0)6 8490-3758
Fax: (0)6 8490-5186

Civil Aviation

There are major international airports at Bologna (G. Marconi), Genoa (Cristoforo Colombo), Milan (Linate and Malpensa), Naples (Capodichino), Pisa (Galileo Galilei), Rome (Leonardo da Vinci), Turin and Venice (Marco Polo). A number of other airports have a small selection of international flights. The national carrier, Alitalia, is 89·3% owned by the state. In 1995 it flew 238·6m. km and carried

20,873,500 passengers. There are a number of other Italian airlines, most notably Meridiana, which flew 21·2m. km and carried 2,522,100 passengers in 1995. The busiest airport is Rome, which in 1996 handled 22,762,967 passengers (12,230,672 on international flights) and 256,300 tonnes of freight. In 1996 Milan Linate was the second busiest for passengers, handling 12,556,207 (6,776,782 on inter-national flights), and Milan Malpensa the second busiest for freight, with 98,000 tonnes.

Alitalia (Linee Aeree Italiane)
Founded 1946. State owned airline with international services world-wide.

Viale Alissandro Marchetti 111, 00148 Roma. Tel: (0)6 7092-780 Fax: (0)6 7093-065

Aero Trasporti Itialiani SpA (ATI)
Founded 1963. Subsidiary of Alitalia operating domestic services and charter flights.

Plazzo ATI, Aeroporto Capodichino, 80144 Napoli.
Tel: (0)81 7091-111 Fax: (0)81 7092-212

Shipping
The mercantile marine in 1995 consisted of 614 vessels of 11·88m. DWT, representing 1·79% of the world's tonnage. 112 vessels (26·42% of tonnage) were registered under foreign flags. Total tonnage registered was 6·82m. GRT, including oil tankers, 2·18m. GRT and container ships, 0·14m. GRT. In 1995, 234,115,000 tonnes of cargo were unloaded, and 48,254,000 were loaded. 2,039,697 passengers embarked and 2,185,645 departed in 1995.

Direzione Generale della Marina Mercantile (General Direction of Merchant Marine)
Via dell'Arte 16, 00144 Roma.

Shipping Association

Confederazione Italiana Armatori (CONFITARMA):

    Founded 1901. Federation of Italian Shipowners.

    Piazza S. Apostoli 66, 00187 Roma. Tel: (0)6 6991-261

Fax: (0)6 6789-473

Telecommunications

There were 25,698,000 main telephone lines in 1997, or 446·8 per
1,000 persons. In 1997 cellular phone subscribers numbered
5,266,094; in 1995 there were 4·8m. PCs and 202,000 fax machines.
There were approximately 2·6m. Internet users in May 1998.

Postal Services

In 1995 there were 14,142 post offices, or 1 for every 4,050 persons.

SOCIAL INSTITUTIONS

Justice

Italy has 1 court of cassation, in Rome, and is divided for the administration of justice into 28 appeal court districts, subdivided into 164
tribunal *circondari* (districts), and these again into about 617 districts
each with its own magistracy (*Pretura*). There are also 90 first degree
assize courts and 28 assize courts of appeal. For civil business,
besides the magistracy above mentioned, *Conciliatori* have jurisdiction
in petty plaints (those to a maximum of 1m. lire).

    2,840,077 crimes were reported in 1997; 552,787 persons were
indicted. In 1997 there were 88,024 persons in prison (6,588 females).

Religion

The treaty between the Holy See and Italy of 11 Feb. 1929, confirmed
by article 7 of the Constitution of the republic, lays down that the

Catholic Apostolic Roman Religion is the only religion of the State. Other creeds are permitted, provided they do not profess principles, or follow rites, contrary to public order or moral behaviour.

The appointment of archbishops and of bishops is made by the Holy See; but the Holy See submits to the Italian Government the name of the person to be appointed in order to obtain an assurance that the latter will not raise objections of a political nature.

Catholic religious teaching is given in elementary and intermediate schools. Marriages celebrated before a Catholic priest are automatically transferred to the civil register. Marriages celebrated by clergy of other denominations must be made valid before a registrar.

There were 47,000,000 Roman Catholics in 1997, 700,000 Moslems and 9,800,000 other (mostly non-religious and atheist).

Italy has a unique religious heritage and the influences of 2000 years of Christianity have permeated every aspect of Italian culture. The Church ceased to be a political power in Italy during the 18th century but the spiritual influence of the church, and Italy's close relationship with the Vatican continues to wield enormous power in all areas of life. The relationship is full of contradictions. Only 25% of Italians now attend mass regularly but while many children are not baptized, first communion remains a popular event, couples still prefer to be married in church and religions festivals and saints' days form the backbone of the Italian holiday schedule. The Vatican has had many feuds with the government and political parties that have proved impossible to win. Communist party members are technically excommunicated although many of them remain fervent Catholics. In the 1920s, the church declared the Italian government ideologically unsound and therefore all its members ineligible for communion (a state of affairs rectified by the Lateran Treaty of 1929 that secularized the state of Italy). In the developed regions of Italy, the people are pragmatic about the more traditional edicts of the Catholic Church.

Despite a religious ban on 'non-natural' birth control, Italy has the one of the lowest birth rates in the world (and one of the most prosperous condom industries). The areas of Emilia Romagna and Umbria have a long anti-priest tradition – there is even a pasta named 'strango-lapreti' or priest-strangler. Away from the developed areas, mainly in the poorer southern regions, attitudes to the church have remained much more traditional. Catholicism, the church and the sacerdotal hierarchy have remained at the heart of most local communities. Italy is tolerant of other religions. 85% of Italians professed to being Catholics in a census taken in the 1980s, but of the remaining 15%, about 500,000 were evangelical Protestants, 140,000 were Jehovah's Witnesses, in addition to which there was a large Jewish community in Rome and small communities of Swiss-Protestants Baptists (the Valdesi) living in Piedmont. The orange robes of the followers of Bhagwan Rajneesh can be seen in major cities. They are known simply as 'arancioni' (little orange people).

For ecclesiastical purposes, Italy comprises the Papal See of Rome, the Patriarchate of Venice, 59 archdioceses, 158 dioceses, two territorial Prelatures and seven territorial Abbacies. Except for two dioceses and one Abbacy that adhere to the Byzantine Rite, all others adhere to the Latin Rite.

Religious Organizations
Conferenza Episcopale Italiana (Bishops Conference)
Circonvallazione Aurelia 50, 00165 Roma. Tel: (0)6 663-981
Fax: (0)6 6623-037

Azione Cattolica Italiana ACI (Catholic Action): Via della Conciliazione 1, 00193 Roma. Tel: (0)6 6868-751 Fax: (0)6 6880-2088
   Italian Catholic Action is the largest of numerous apostolic lay organisations with a total membership of over 1m.

Federazione delle Chiese Evangeliche in Italia (Federation of Protestant Churches in Italy)
Via Firenze 38, 00184 Roma. Tel: (0)6 4825-120 Fax: (0)6 4828-728
The Federation represents more than 50,000 members.

Esercito della Salvezza (Salvation Army): Via degli Apuli 39, 00185 Roma. Tel: (0)6 4462-614 Fax: (0)6 490-078
There are 15 regional centres of the Salvation Army in Italy.

Union of Italian Jewish Communities: Longotavere Sanzio 9, 00153 Roma. Tel: (0)6 5803-667 Fax: (0)6 5899-569.
Represents 21 Jewish Communities in Italy (and Malta).

Rabbinical Council: Via Catalana 1A, Roma.
Headquarters of the Chief Rabbi.

Education

5 years of primary and 3 years of secondary education are compulsory from the age of 6. In 1997–98 there were 26,122 pre-school institutions with 1,594,062 pupils (including 13,624 state-run institutions with 917,881pupils); 19,418 primary schools with 2,816,161 pupils (including 17,544 state schools with 2,618,077 pupils); 8,829 compulsory secondary schools (*scuole medie*) with 1,806,613 pupils (including 8,049 state schools with 1,740,355 pupils); and 7,848 higher secondary schools with 2,628,377 pupils (including 5,967 state-run with 2,449,347 pupils). Numbers of teachers: Pre-primary institutions, 1996–97, 121,062; primary schools, 1996–97, 281,326; compulsory secondary schools, 1996–97, 230,945; higher secondary schools, 1996–97, 315,920.

Higher secondary education is subdivided into classical (*ginnasio* and classical *liceo*), scientific (scientific *liceo*), language lyceum, professional institutes and technical education: agricultural, industrial, commercial, technical, nautical institutes, institutes for surveyors, institutes for girls (5-year course) and teacher-training institutes (4-year course).

In 1995–96 there were 47 universities, 2 universities of Italian studies for foreigners and 3 specialized universities (commerce; education; Roman Catholic), 3 polytechnical university institutes and 7 other specialized university institutes: (architecture; bio-medicine; modern languages; naval studies; oriental studies; social studies; teacher training). In 1996–97 there were 1,672,330 university students and 58,111 academic staff.

Adult literacy rate, 1995, 98·1% (male 98·6%; female 97·6%).

In 1993 total expenditure on education came to 5·2% of GNP and represented 9·0% of total government expenditure.

Health

The provision of health services is a regional responsibility, but they are funded by central government. Medical consultations are free, but a portion of prescription costs are payable. In 1996 there were 1,005 public hospitals with 274,282 beds and 782 private hospitals with 81,457 beds. In 1996 there were 110,261 doctors in public hospitals and 264,774 auxiliary medical personnel.

Welfare

Social expenditure is made up of transfers which the central public departments, local departments and social security departments make to families. Payment is principally for pensions, family allowances and health services. Expenditure on subsidies, public assistance to various classes of people and people injured by political events or national disasters are also included.

Public pensions are indexed to prices; 21,551,751 pensions were paid in 1996 (18,423,597 private sector, 3,128,154 public sector). Current social security expenditure in 1996 was 316,842,000m. lire, of which 301,451,000m. lire were paid out in benefits. Social contributions totalled 227,991,000m. lire. In 1997 pension expenditure, which was 15% of GDP, was one of the highest in Europe.

CULTURE

Bologna is one of nine European Cities of Culture in the year 2000, and has as its theme 'Information and Communication'. The other Cities of Culture are Avignon (France), Bergen (Norway), Brussels (Belgium), Helsinki (Finland), Kraków (Poland), Prague (Czech Republic), Reykjavík (Iceland) and Santiago de Compostela (Spain). The title attracts large European Union grants.

Broadcasting

Broadcasting is regulated by the Public Radio-Television Administration Council. Questions were raised over the impartiality of state-owned *Radiotelevisione Italiana (RAI)* during the election campaign of 1994. As a result, following a referendum in 1995, RAI was partially privatized. There are 15 national and about 820 local private TV networks. In 1995 there were 47m. television sets (colour by PAL). In 1996, 16,114,572 television licences were bought.

Radiotelevisione Italiana (RAI): Viale Mazzini 14, 00195 Roma. Tel: (0)6 38781 Fax: (0)6 3226-070 Web: www.ai.it

Broadcasts 3 TV channels: RAI Uno, RAI Due (both broadcasting general interest programmes), RAI Tre (programmes with a cultural emphasis plus regional news) and 3 radio channels.

Rundfunkanstalt Südtirol (RAS): Europaallee 164A, 39100 Bozen. Tel: (0)471 932 933 Fax: (0)471 200 378

Transmits TV and radio German-language programmes from Austria, Germany and Switzerland to the Alto-Adige (South Tyrol).

Press

Italy has approximately 115 dailies (84 are general information) and 569 weeklies. The combined circulation of the dailies (including unsold copies) is 2,177,409 every day, and of the weeklies 907,091. Several of the papers are owned or supported by political parties. The church and various economic groups exert strong right of centre influence on editorial opinion. Most newspapers are regional but La Repubblica, Corriere della Sera, La Stampa and Il Giorno are the most important of those papers that are nationally circulated.

News Agencies

Agenzia Nazionale Stampa Associata

Founded 1945. 22 regional offices in Italy and 90 branches worldwide.

Via della Dataria 94, 00187 Roma. Tel: (0)6 6774-310
Fax: (0)6 6782-408

Associated Press (AP) (USA)

Piazza Grazioli 5, 00186 Roma. Tel: (0)6 6789-936
Web: www.ap.org

Reuters (UK)

Via della Cordonata 7, 00187 Roma. Tel: (0)6 6782-501
Fax: (0)6 794-248 Web: www.reuters.it

United Press (UPI) (USA)

Via delle Mercede 55, 00187 Roma. Tel: (0)6 6795-747
Fax: (0)6 6781-540

Inter Press Service (IPS)

Via Panisperna 207, 00184 Roma. Tel: (0)6 485-692
Fax: (0)6 4817-877

Newspapers

La Repubblica

Founded 1976. Left wing daily newspaper.

Piazza Indipendenza 11B, 00185 Roma. Tel: (0)6 49821

Fax: (0)6 4982-2923

Corriere della Sera

Founded 1876. Independent daily newspaper with weekly
supplements.

Via Solferino 28, 10121 Milano. Tel: (0)2 6339. Fax: (0)2 2900-9668

La Stampa

Founded 1868. Independent daily newspaper.

Via Marenco 32, 10126 Torino. Tel: (0)11 65681

Il Giornale

Founded 1974. Independent, controlled by staff.

Via Gaetano Negri 4, 20123 Milano. Tel: (0)2 85661

Fax: (0)2 8566-327

Il Giorno

Piazza Cavour 2, 20121 Milano. Tel: (0)2 77681

Periodicals

Panorama: Arnaldo Mondadori Editatore SpA. Via Marconi 27,
20090 Segrate (Milano). Tel: (0)2 7543 Fax: (0)2 7542-2769
Weekly current affairs.

Oggi: Gruppo Riozzoli. Corso Garibaldi 86, 20121 Milano.
Tel: (0)2 665-941

Illustrated weekly, topical, literary magazine.

Gente: Vilae Sarca 235, 20126 Milano. Tel: (0)2 27751
Weekly illustrated political, cultural and current events.

Sports Newspapers

Tutosport: Corso Svizzera 185, 10147 Torino. Tel: (0)11 77731
Corriere dello Sport: Piazza Independenza 11b, 00185 Roma.
Tel: (0)6 49921 Fax: (0)6 4992-690

Book Publishers

Bompiana

Founded 1929. Subjects include fiction and general non-fiction.
Via Mecenate 91, 20138 Milano. Tel: (0)2 50951
Fax: (0)2 50952-058

Nuova Casa Editrice Licionio Cappelli GEM srl

Founded 1851. Subjects include fiction, art, biography, history,
medicine, philosophy, poetry, psychology, religion, science and
sociology.
Via Farini 14, 40124 Bologna. Tel (0)51 239060 Fax: (0)51 239286

Garzanti Editore

Founded 1861. Subjects include fiction, literature, art, poetry, biogra-
phy and political science.
Via Newton 18A, 20148 Milano. Tel: (0)2 487941
Fax (0)2 76009-233

Giunti Publishing Group

Founded 1840. Subjects include fiction, literature, art, history,
psychology and science. Publishers of National Geographical Society
books.
Via Bolognese 165, 50139 Firenze. Tel: (0)55 66791
Fax (0)55 66792-98

Longanesi & C. SpA

Founded 1946. Subjects include fiction, art, biography, history,
poetry, philosophy, religion, education and science.
Corso Italia 13, 20122 Milano. Tel: (0)2 8692640 Fax (0)2 72000-306

Arnoldo Mondadori Editore SpA

Founded 1907. Subjects include fiction, art, poetry, biography, history, philosophy, psychology, religion and science.

Via Mondadori, 20090 Segrate (Milano). Tel: (0)2 75421
Fax (0)2 75422-886

Gruppo Ugo Musia Editore SpA

Founded 1922. Subjects include fiction, art, poetry, biography, education, history, religion, philosophy and science.

Via Tadino 29, 20124 Milano. Tel: (0)2 29403-030
Fax (0)2 39535-557

Societa Editrice Internazionale – SEI

Founded 1908. Subjects include literature, education, history, philosophy, religion and psychology.

Corso Regina Margherita 176, 10152 Torino. Tel: (0)11 52271
Fax (0)11 5211320

Sperling e Kupfer Editori SpA

Founded 1899. Subjects include fiction and general non-fiction.

Via Borgonuovo 24, 20121 Milano. Tel: (0)2 290341
Fax (0)2 6590290

SPORT

Although the health and fitness boom of the 1980s produced an outbreak of health and fitness centres, tennis clubs and golf courses in and around the major cities of Italy, the popular sports are mostly spectator ones – football, motor racing and cycling. Football ('Il Calcio') was introduced into Italy at the turn of the 20th century by British industrialists who imported factory sports clubs as part of the ethos of workers welfare. The evolution of sport in Italy was greatly accelerated by the fascist government in the years leading up to the war when a number of large stadia were built. In 1960 Rome played host to the Olympic Games which led to the building of Nervi's Palazzo and Palazzetta dello Sport in Rome. On the whole, training facilities for the serious athlete are not easy to find in Italy.

Italians are fanatical football fans. Their country won the World Cup in 1934, 1938 and 1982 and regional clubs have a tradition of signing the most flamboyant and expensive players from all over the world (Argentina's Maradona played for Naples and England's 'Gazza' played for Lazio of Rome). Until 1996, Italian clubs were officially non-profit organizations but they have now been allowed to raise funds to improve facilities and some clubs are even listed on the Italian stock exchange (a club must show a profit for three consecutive years in order to qualify for stock market flotation). Nearly every man and boy plays football at some time in local clubs and leagues.

Motor racing is Italy's second most popular sport. Speed suits the Italian temperament and through the years Italy's motor industry has produced some of the world's most successful racing cars including Ferrari and Bugatti. The Mille Miglia and the Targa Florio (which takes place in Sicily) are two famous Italian motor races and the motor racing circuit at Monza is known the world over.

Italy makes several excellent racing bicycles including Bianchi and Campagnolo and the Italians have their own version of the 'Tour de France' – the Giro d'Italia which takes place every year.

The Italian Alps and the Apennines attract large numbers of visitors every year, not only in winter for the winter sports (Italy has produced some world-class skiers including the Olympic gold medallist Alberto Tomba), but also in summer for hiking and mountain climbing. In recent years, professional basketball has caught on as a popular sport and players are being imported from the United States and elsewhere.

TOURISM

In 1997, 56,370,381 foreigners visited Italy. They included French,
9,726,229; Germans, 8,441,385; Swiss, 8,164,696; Austrians,
5,872,836. Foreign tourist revenue was 50,847,000m. lire in 1997.

Dipartimento del Tourismo (Department of Tourism)
Presidenza del Consiglio dei Ministri, Via della Ferratella in Laterano
51, 00184 Roma. Tel: (0)6 77321 Fax: (0)6 7001-992

Ente Nazionale Italiano per il Turismo (ENIT)
(National Tourist Board)
Founded 1919. Central National Tourist Board. There are over 2,000
local tourist associations throughout Italy.
   Vie Marghera 2, 00185 Roma. Tel: (0)6 49711
Fax: (0)6 4963-379

Italian Tourist Offices in the United Kingdom and the
United States of America
UK
Italian State Tourist Board (ENIT) 1 Princes Street, London W1R 8AY.
Tel: (0)20 7408-1254 Fax: (0)20 7493-6695
Email: enitlond@globalnet.co.uk

USA
Italian Government Travel Office (New York) 630 Fifth Ave.,
New York, NY 10111. Tel: (212) 245-4822 Fax: (212) 586-9249

Italian Government Travel Office (Illinois)
500 N. Michigan Ave., Chicago, IL 60611. Tel: (312) 644-0990
Fax: (312) 644-3019

Italian Government Travel Office (California)
12400 Wilshire Blvd., Los Angeles, CA 90025. Tel: (310) 820-0098
Fax: (310) 820-6357

Tourist Information Websites

www.enit.it www.initaly.com www.it
www.itwg.com www.business-travel-net.com

Central Hotel Reservations

Central reservation numbers of hotel chains/booking services
represented in the UK.

Best Western: 0800 393 130. Web: www.bestwestern.com
Hilton International: 0345 581 595. Web: www.hilton.com
Holiday Inn: 0800 897 121. Web: www.basshotels.com
ITT Sheraton: 0800 353 535. Web: www.starwood.com
Jolly Hotels: 0800 731 0470. Web: www.jollyhotels.it

Central Car Hire

Avis: Web: www.avis.com. (0)6 419-948
Hertz: Web: www.hertz.com 0199 112-211
Budget: Web: www.budgetrentacar.com (0)6 2291-530
Thrifty: Web: www.thrifty.com 0990 168-238 (UK number)
Europcar: Web: www.europcar.com (0)2 7039-9700

Millennium Events and Festivals

While the main focus of attention for what the Pope has dubbed
'The Great Jubilee' will be on Rome and the Vatican, plans to celebrate the turn of the new millennium are underway elsewhere in Italy.
Bologna was the site of the first university in Europe and in 2000 it will
be one of the nine European Cities of Culture. Bologna's Theme for
2000 is Communication, and as part of its programme the city will be
opening a number of new or refurbished museums and cultural
institutions including the Mediatheque – designed to be the largest
library in Italy – with a multi-media project presided over by Umberto
Eco. Other projects in Bologna include the opening of a new Museum
of Jewish Culture, the restoration of the Palace of King Enzo, and the

Podestà. A derelict area around the former tobacco factory is to be converted into a Centre for the Visual Arts, and a National Library and Documentation Centre for Women is being created. As well as many special shows and exhibitions, there will be programmes of religious art for pilgrims on their way to Rome.

The historic port of Genoa will be one of the starting points for the Tall Ships 2000 race and, to coincide with this, will present a series of maritime events and exhibitions during 20–23 April 2000. In Turin, the cathedral is planning a special showing of the Turin Shroud (the cloth said to have been wrapped around the body of Christ at his burial). The Shroud has not been exhibited since 1987 when it was seen by 3m. visitors. The Italian government has allocated £18m. for cultural events and projects for the millennium including four major exhibitions in the newly renovated stables of the Quirinale (Rome's Presidential Palace). Funds will also be made available to the Rome opera, to young artists all over Italy and for the opening of new cultural sites.

For more information:

Bologna: Bologna 2000, via Oberdan 24, 40126 Bologna.

Tel: (0)51 204-653 Fax: (0)51 268-636

Email: Bologna2000@comune.bologna.it

Web: www.comune.bologna.it/Bologna2000

Rome Information: Web: www.roma2000.com

For Vatican City Millennium events and celebrations see under 'Vatican City' on page 183.

Annual Festivals

Every town and village has its own saint's day festivities and local closing times may not correspond to the national holidays given below. Each local tourist office will have details of the festivals in each region and what follows is a table of some of the larger and national festivals. For further information please visit the local tourist office or write to:

The Italian Government Travel Office (ENT): Ente Nazionale Italiano per il Turismo (ENIT):

Via Marghera 2, 00185 Rome. Tel: (0)6 49711 Fax: (0)6 4963-379
Information Websites: www.enit.it www.initaly.com www.it

17 Jan.	Feast of St. Anthony	Rome
30–31 Jan.	St. Orso Fair (Local crafts)	Aosta
Late Jan./ Early Feb.	Carnival (Mardi Gras)	Viareggio
3 Feb.	Festa di Fiori di Mandorlo (Almond Blossom fair)	Agrigento
Feb.	Masked Carnival (ends Shrove Tuesday)	Venice
Feb.	Bacchanalian Carnival of the Gnocco	Verona

Holy Week and Easter (at the end of Lent just before Easter and all over the Easter period there are religious processions and celebrations all over Italy.)

Easter Day	Scoppio del Carro (a dove slides along a wire from the high altar of the Cathedral into the piazza and ignites a display of fireworks)	Florence
21 April	Anniversario della Fondazione di Roma (Anniversary of Rome's foundation)	Rome
25 April	Festival of San Marco	Venice
Late April/ Early July	Music and cultural festival	Florence
Early May	Festival of the miracle of St. Januarius	Naples
First week of May	Calendimaggio (May Day celebrations)	Assisi
7–10 May	Feast of St. Nicholas processions and celebrations when statue of the saint is taken out to sea	Bari

15 May	Corso di Ceri (candle race)	Gubbio
1–14 June	Mostra Internazionale del Nuovo Cinema	Pesaro
First 2 weeks June (even years only)	Biennial Arts Festival	Venice
24 June	Feast Day of St. John	Genoa, Turin and Florence
29 June	Feast of Sts. Peter and Paul	Rome
Last week June/First week July	International festival of Music drama and dance	Spoleto
Early July/ Late Aug.	Summer drama festival and opera in the Amphitheatre	Verona
Early July	Palio delle Contrade (mounted race around the piazza between historic Siennese families)	Siena
11 July	Feast Day of St. Rosalia	Palermo
Late Aug./ Early Sept.	International Film Festival (on the Lido)	Venice
1st Sunday in Sept.	Regata Storica (historic Regatta on the Grand Canal)	Venice
1 Sept.	Giostra del Saraceno (Joust of the Saracens)	Arezzo
7 Sept.	Feast of the Rificolone (Coloured paper lanterns) with musical and folk events	Florence
7–8 Sept.	Feast of the Nativity of the Virgin	Loreto
2nd Friday Sept.	Partita di Scacchi (life-size chess game)	Marostica
Mid-Sept.	Wine Festival and Palio horse race	Asti
2nd Sunday in Sept.	Palio della Balestra in medieval costume	Sansepolcro

13/14 Sept.	Illuminations, cross bow competitions, Palio (the famous horse race)	Lucca
19 Sept.	Feast Day of St. Gennaro	Naples
2nd & 3rd Sundays Sept.	Quintana Games in 17th century costumes	Foligno
Mid-Sept.– mid-Oct. (odd years only)	Biennial Antique Fair	Florence
1 Oct.	Investiture of the City Regents	San Marino
4 Oct.	Feast Day of St. Petronio	Bologna
7 Dec.	Feast Day of St. Ambrose	Milan
10 Dec.	Feast of the Translation of the Santa Casa (Holy House)	Loreto

National Public Holidays

1 Jan.	New Year's Day
6 Jan.	Epiphany
25 April	Liberation Day
March/April	Easter Day
1 May	May Day
Sunday nearest 2 June	Anniversary of the Republic
15 Aug.	Assumption of the Virgin Mary
1 Nov.	All Saints Day
8 Dec.	Immaculate Conception
25 Dec.	Christmas Day
26 Dec.	Boxing or St. Stephen's Day

Many towns also have holidays on the feast days of their patron saints – local tourist offices will have dates.

ETIQUETTE

Social

Italian people are relaxed and friendly and easy to get to know socially. Even if you are not introduced to each person in a group it is polite to shake hands with everyone. When addressing someone you do not know in Italian, it courteous to use the third person singular (i.e. 'would she like a cake' rather than 'would you like a cake'). Although Italian manners are quite informal, it is polite to greet people with 'Buongiorno Signora' (Signore for men and Signorina for young women) with or without their name and to use 'Signora' etc. during the conversation.

Italians tend to entertain at home, although much of informal social life is spent meeting and chatting in cafés.

Business

The Italian business day starts early and ends late with a long break in the middle of the day. Most Italian businessmen take a long lunch, often at home, so you may find meetings scheduled either very early in the morning or late in the evening. It is considered polite to address business people by their title if you know it (i.e. Dirretore, Dottore/Dottoressa, Ingegnere, Professore/Professoressa, etc.) and use it liberally throughout the conversation. Fashion is important in Italy and most men dress formally in suit and tie and often carry a kind of handbag/leather pouch so as not to spoil the line of their suit with wallets etc. This should not be considered effeminate. Women are also very well dressed usually in dresses or suits with skirts rather than trousers. Italian legalities in business are rather complicated, so be sure to have your own local legal adviser if negotiating contracts.

DIPLOMATIC REPRESENTATIVES

Of Italy in Great Britain (14 Three Kings Yard, Davies Street, London, W1Y 2EH)
Ambassador: Dr Paolo Galli.

Of Great Britain in Italy (Via XX Settembre 80A, 00187, Rome)
Ambassador: Tom Richardson, CMG.

Of Italy in the USA (1601 Fuller St., NW, Washington, D.C., 20009)
Ambassador: Ferdinando Salleo.

Of the USA in Italy (Via Veneto 119/A, Rome)
Ambassador: Thomas M. Foglietta.

Of Italy to the United Nations
Ambassador: Francesco Paolo Fulci.

FOREIGN EMBASSIES AND CONSULATES

Australia: Via Alessandria 215, 00198 Rome. Tel: (0)6 852-721
Fax: (0)6 8527-2300

Austria: Via G.B. Pergolesi 3, 00198 Rome. Tel: (0)6 8558-241
Fax: (0)6 8543-286

Belgium: Via dei Monti Paroli 49, 00197 Rome. Tel: (0)6 3609-511
Fax: (0)6 3236-935

Canada: Via G.B. de Rossi 27, 00161 Rome. Tel: (0)6 445-981
Fax: (0)6 4459-8750

China (People's Republic): Via Bruxelles 56, 00198 Rome.
Tel: (0)6 8448-186

Denmark: Via dei Monti Paroli 50, 00197 Rome. Tel: (0)6 3200-441
Fax: (0)6 3610-290

France: Piazza Farnese 67, 00186 Rome. Tel: (0)6 686-011
Fax: (0)6 6860-1360

Germany: Via Po 25c, 00198 Rome. Tel: (0)6 884-741
Fax: (0)6 8547-956

Greece: Via Mercadente 36, 00198 Rome. Tel: (0)6 8549-630
Fax: (0)6 8432-579-27

Holy See: Via Po 27–29, 00198 Rome. Tel: (0)6 8546-287
Fax: (0)6 8549-725

Ireland
Largo del Nazareno 3, 00187 Rome. Tel: (0)6 6782-541
Fax: (0)6 6792-354

Japan: Via Quintino Sella 60, 00187 Rome. Tel: (0)6 4877-991
Fax: (0)6 4873-316

Luxembourg: Via Guerrieri 3, 00153 Rome. Tel: (0)6 5780-456
Fax: (0)6 5744-874

Netherlands: Via Michele Mercati 8, 00197 Rome. Tel: (0)6 3221-141
Fax: (0)6 3221-440

New Zealand: Via Zara 28, 00198 Rome. Tel: (0)6 4402-928
Fax: (0)6 4402-984

Norway: Via delle Terme Deciane 7, 00153 Rome. Tel: (0)6 5755-833
Fax: (0)6 5742-115

Portugal: Via Giacinta Pezzana 9, 00197 Rome. Tel: (0)6 878-016

Russia: Via Gaeta 5, 00185 Rome. Tel: (0)6 4743-989

South Africa: Via Tanaro 14, 00198 Rome. Tel: (0)6 8410-794
Fax: (0)6 8550-051

Spain: Palazzo Borghese, Largo Fontanella Borghese 19, 00186
Rome. Tel: (0)6 6878-172 Fax: (0)6 6872-256

Sweden: Piazza Rio de Janeiro 3, 00161 Rome. Tel: (0)6 4423-1459

Switzerland: Via Barnaba Oriani 61, 00197 Rome. Tel: (0)6 8083-641
Fax: (0)6 8088-510

Turkey: Via Palestro 28, 00185 Rome. Tel: (0)6 4469-933
Fax: (0)6 4941-526

UK: Via Settembre 80A, 00187 Rome. Tel: (0)6 4825-551
Fax: (0)6 4873-324

USA: Via Vittorio Veneto 119A, 00187 Rome. Tel: (0)6 4674
Fax: (0)6 4674-2356

LIBRARIES

In 1995 Italy's libraries held a combined 112,492,000 volumes and
were utilized by 9,261,185 registered users.

FURTHER READING

Istituto Nazionale di Statistica. *Annuario Statistico Italiano.* – *Compendio
Statistico Italiano.* (Annual). – *Italian Statistical Abstract* (Annual). –
Bollettino Mensile di Statistica (Monthly).

Absalom, R., *Italy since 1880: a Nation in the Balance?* Harlow, 1995

Baldassarri, M. (ed.) *The Italian Economy: Heaven or Hell?* London, 1993

Clark, M., *Modern Italy 1871–1982.* London, 1984

Di Scala, S. M., *Italy from Revolution to Republic: 1700 to the Present.* Boulder (CO), 1995

Duggan, C., *A Concise History of Italy.* Cambridge University Press, 1994

Frei, M., *Italy: the Unfinished Revolution.* London, 1996

Furlong, P., *Modern Italy: Representation and Reform.* London, 1994

Gilbert, M. *Italian Revolution: the Ignominious End of Politics, Italian Style.* Boulder (CO), 1995

Ginsborg, P., *A History of Contemporary Italy: Society and Politics, 1943–1988.* London, 1990

Gundie, S. and Parker, S. (eds.) *The New Italian Republic: from the Fall of the Berlin Wall to Berlusconi.* London, 1995

Hearder, H., *Italy: a Short History.* Cambridge University Press, 1991

McCarthy, P., *The Crisis of the Italian State: from the Origins of the Cold War to the Fall of Berlusconi.* London, 1996

OECD, *OECD Economic Surveys 1998–99: Italy.* Paris, 1998

Putnam, R. *et al., Making Democracy Work: Civic Traditions in Modern Italy.* Princeton Univ. Press, 1993

Richards, C., *The New Italians.* London, 1994

Smith, D. M., *Modern Italy: A Political History.* Yale University Press, 1997

Sponza, L. and Zancani, D., *Italy* [Bibliography]. Oxford and Santa Barbara (CA), 1995

Volcansek, Mary L., *Constitutional Politics in Italy.* Macmillan, 1999

National statistical office: Istituto Nazionale di Statistica (ISTAT), 16 Via Cesare Balbo, 00184 Rome. *Web:* www.istat.it/

National library: Biblioteca Nazionale Centrale, Vittorio Emanuele II, Viale Castro Pretorio, Rome.

Web site for general information on government, policies, etc. www.italyemb.org

TOURIST AND HOTEL GUIDES

Andrews, R., Brown, J. and Dunford, M., *Sicily: the Rough Guide*. Rough Guides, 1999

Belford, R., Dunford, M. and Woolfrey, C., *Italy: the Rough Guide*. Rough Guides, 1999

Eyewitness Travel Guide to Sardinia. Dorling Kindersley, 1998

Fodor's 99 Italy (Fodor's Gold Guides). Fodor's Travel Publications, 1999

Gillman, H., and Simonis, D., *Lonely Planet: Italy*. Lonely Planet Publications, 1999

Johansens Recommended Hotels: Europe and the Mediterranean 2000. Johansens, 1999

Let's Go: Italy. Macmillan, 1999

Michelin Green Guide: Italy. Michelin, 1998

Michelin Green Guide: Sicily. Michelin, 1998

Michelin Red Guide Italy 1999: Hotels – Restaurants. Michelin

Rockwood, C. (ed.), *Fodor's Florence, Tuscany and Umbria (Fodor's Gold Guides)*. Fodor's Travel Publications, 1999

VATICAN CITY (STATO DELLA CITTÀ DEL VATICANO)

The Vatican is the seat and headquarters of the Catholic Church and the home of the Pope. It is a self-contained sovereign state within the city of Rome. Medieval and Renaissance walls surround it on three sides; the fourth side is bounded by the Basilica of St. Peter's (Basilica di S. Pietro) and St. Peter's Square (Piazza S. Pietro).

The Vatican owes its origins to the gift of Pepin the Short to Pope Stephen II at the creation of the Papal States in the 8th century. The Vatican remained thus until 1870 when Italy was united into one Kingdom with Rome as its capital. The Papal States (or what remained of them) were annexed by the new Italian government and the pontiffs decided that rather than acknowledge the new united Kingdom of Italy (despite guarantees of the future judicial and financial status of the Vatican) they would shut themselves off behind the Vatican walls. This state of affairs lasted until 1929 when the Fascist government under Mussolini drew up a treaty between the Italian government and the Vatican which was signed on 11 Feb. and ratified later that year on 7 June. Under the terms of this treaty, the independence and sovereignty of the Vatican was fully recognized and the government agreed to make financial restitution for the losses suffered by the Church in 1870. In return, the Pope formally recognized the sovereignty of the Kingdom of Italy.

The Pope is head of State and appoints the members of the Vatican governmental organs. Order is maintained by a small force of gendarmes and the Swiss Guards, who wear flamboyant uniform designed by Michelangelo, and who are dedicated to the personal protection of the Pope. Diplomatic representatives are sent and received but although foreign representatives, ambassadors etc are accredited to the Holy See, they actually live and have their offices in Rome.

The Vatican contains some of the finest works of art in Italy, on display in St. Peter's Basilica, the Vatican Museum and Library (the museum contains the Sistine Chapel, painted by Michelangelo for Pope Julius II between 1508 and 1512), the Pinacoteca and the Vatican Gardens.

As well as its own peacekeeping force, the Vatican has its own post office, radio station, television station and newspaper. It mints its own coins (Italian lire but with the Pope's face) and issues its own stamps.

TERRITORY AND POPULATION

The area of the Vatican City is 44 ha (108·7 acres). It includes the
Piazza di San Pietro (St Peter's Square), which is to remain normally
open to the public and subject to the powers of the Italian police.
It has its own railway station (for freight only), postal facilities, coins
and radio. Twelve buildings in and outside Rome enjoy extra-
territorial rights, including the Basilicas of St John Lateran, St Mary
Major and St Paul without the Walls, the Pope's summer villa at Castel
Gandolfo and a further Vatican radio station on Italian soil. *Radio
Vaticana* broadcasts an extensive service in 34 languages from the
transmitters in the Vatican City and in Italy.

The Vatican City has about 900 inhabitants.

CONSTITUTION AND GOVERNMENT

The Vatican City State is governed by a Commission appointed by the
Pope. The reason for its existence is to provide an extra-territorial,
independent base for the Holy See, the government of the Roman
Catholic Church. The Pope exercises sovereignty and has absolute
legislative, executive and judicial powers. The judicial power is
delegated to a tribunal in the first instance, to the Sacred Roman
Rota in appeal and to the Supreme Tribunal of the Signature in final
appeal.

The Pope is elected by the College of Cardinals, meeting in
secret conclave. The election is by scrutiny and requires a two-thirds
majority.

CURRENT ADMINISTRATION

Supreme Pontiff: **John Paul II** (Karol Wojtyła), born at Wadowice near Kraków, Poland, 18 May 1920. Archbishop of Kraków 1964–78, created Cardinal in 1967; elected Pope 16 Oct. 1978, inaugurated 22 Oct. 1978.

Pope John Paul II was the first non-Italian to be elected since Pope Adrian VI (a Dutchman) in 1522.

Secretary of State: Cardinal Angelo Sodano.

Secretary for Relations with Other States: Jean-Louis Tauran.

ECONOMY

Performance

Real GDP growth was 3·0% in 1995 (2·2% in 1994 but −1·2% in 1993).

Budget

Revenues in 1994 were US$175·5m. and expenditures US$175m.

CULTURE

Press

L'Osservatore Romano

Founded in July 1861 and originally published to defend the Catholic Church after the proclamation of the Kingdom of Italy in 1861, the paper is now the official voice of the Vatican, publishing weekly editions in French, Italian, English (since 1968), Spanish, Portuguese and German and monthly in Polish.

00121 Vatican City. Tel: (0)6698 99390 Fax: (0)6698 85252
Email: ornet@ossrom.va   Web: www.vatican.va

Broadcasting

Vatican Radio

Founded in Feb. 1931. 00120 Vatican City. Tel: (0)6698 83551
Fax: (0)6698 84565

email: sedoc@vatradio.va Web: www.vatican.va

Television

CTV

Founded in 1983, its principal aim is to spread the universal message of the Catholic Church through the gospels and to document the pastoral activities of the Pope.

Via del Pellegrino, 00120 Vatican City. Tel: (0)6698 85467 or (0)6698 85233 Fax: (0)6698 85192

Email: ctv@ctv.va Web: www.vatican.va

ROMAN CATHOLIC CHURCH

The Roman Pontiff (in orders a Bishop, but in jurisdiction held to be by divine right the centre of all Catholic unity, and consequently Pastor and Teacher of all Christians) has for advisers and coadjutors the Sacred College of Cardinals, consisting in Nov. 1996 of 167 Cardinals appointed by him from senior ecclesiastics who are either the bishops of important Sees or the heads of departments at the Holy See. In addition to the College of Cardinals, the Pope has created a 'Synod of Bishops'. This consists of the Patriarchs and certain Metropolitans of the Catholic Church of Oriental Rite, of elected representatives of the national episcopal conferences and religious orders of the world, of the Cardinals in charge of the Roman Congregations and of other persons nominated by the Pope. The Synod meets as and when decided by the Pope. The last Synod (on the formation of priests) met in Oct. 1990.

The central administration of the Roman Catholic Church is carried on by a number of permanent committees called Sacred Congregations, each composed of a number of Cardinals and diocesan bishops (both appointed for 5-year periods), with Consultors and Officials. Besides the Secretariat of State and the Second Section of the Secretariat of State (Section for Relations with States) there are now 9 Sacred Congregations, viz.: Doctrine, Oriental Churches, Bishops, the Sacraments and Divine Worship, Clergy, Religious, Catholic Education, Evangelization of the Peoples and Causes of the Saints. Pontifical Councils have replaced some of the previously designated Secretariats and Prefectures and now represent the Laity, Christian Unity, the Family, Justice and Peace, Cor Unum, Migrants, Health Care Workers, Interpretation of Legislative Texts, Inter-Religious Dialogue, Culture, Preserving the Patrimony of Art and History, and a new Commission, for Latin America. There are also various Offices. The Pontifical Academy of Sciences was revived in 1936. The director of the Vatican Bank (Istituto per le Opere di Religione) is Giovanni Bodio.

MILLENNIUM EVENTS

The Vatican will be the religious focal point for the world's Catholics as the church celebrates the 2000th birthday of the Christian religion. Italy (and especially Rome) will be celebrating the new millennium with a mix of sacred and secular activities. The Vatican (and Rome) is expecting up to 30m. pilgrim-visitors during the year. Building, reconstruction, restoration and renovation is going on all over the city of Rome and in the Vatican. The Basilica of St. Peter's façade has been covered by the largest single piece of scaffolding ever erected. The Vatican has commissioned the American architect, Richard

Meier, to build a new church – the Church of the Year 2000 in Rome
– and has also commissioned the Russian artist, Alexander
Kornoukhov, to create a new 'Mosaic for the Millennium' in the Holy
See's Redemptoris Major Chapel. High-tech 'pilgrim cards' will be
issued by the Vatican to visitors, each carrying a chip enabling them
to book visits and use the telephone and transport systems. The
cards, designed to cut down on the need to carry cash, will also carry
information on the visitor's identity, hotel reservations and travel
plans. 60,000 volunteers have been drafted in to guide pilgrims
around Rome. The Vatican's Millennium celebrations are intended
to last from 24 Dec. 1999 (Christmas Eve) right through to 6 Jan. 2001
(Epiphany). The Pope will symbolically open the Holy Door with a silver hammer (the door is the one nearest to the Vatican, on the right
hand side of the façade of St. Peter's. It is normally bricked up and
only opened during Jubilee years). The Pope is also planning to
deliver a blessing every day during the Great Jubilee year to the
crowds in the Piazza. 29 Jubilee days are being planned for different
groups of people, (artists, children, teachers, scientists, workers,
politicians etc.). On 8 March 2000 the Pope is expected to ask pardon
for past errors of the Church including the Inquisition.

More details and information from:
Great Jubilee 2000: 00129 Vatican City. Tel: (0)6698 82828
Fax: (0)6698 81961 Web: www.vatican.va
(For more information of Millennium events in Rome and Italy see
under Millennium Events on page 168.)

DIPLOMATIC REPRESENTATIVES

In its diplomatic relations with foreign countries the Holy See is represented by the Secretariat of State and the Second Section (Relations

with States) of the Council for Public Affairs of the Church. It maintains permanent observers to the UN.

Of the Holy See in Great Britain (54 Parkside, London, SW19 5NE)
Apostolic Nuncio: Archbishop Pablo Puente.

Of Great Britain at the Holy See (91 Via Dei Condotti, I–00187 Rome).
Ambassador: Mark E. Pellew, LVO.

Of the Holy See in the USA (3339 Massachusetts Ave., NW, Washington, D.C.,20008).
Apostolic Nuncio: Agostino Cacciavillan.

Of the USA at the Holy See (Villa Domiziana, Via Delle Terme Deciane 26, 00153 Rome).
Ambassador: Corinne C. Boggs.

TRAVELLERS INFORMATION

Pilgrim Tourist Information Office
Papal Audiences. Papal audiences (usually held weekly on Wednesday mornings) can be requested by applying in writing.
Prefettura Della Casa Pontifica, 00120 Città del Vaticano.
Tel: (0)6698 83017
Piazza S. Pietro. Tel: (0)6698 84466 or (0)6698 84866
Fax: (0)6698 85100

Vatican Post Office
The Vatican has its own postal system and issues its own stamps.
It has 2 locations on the Piazza S. Pietro.

Landmarks

Basilica di San Pietro/Piazza di San Pietro (St. Peter's Basilica/ St. Peter's Square)

In 324 AD Constantine, the first Christian Emperor, founded a Basilica here on the spot where St. Peter was buried after his martyrdom at the hands of the Roman Emperor Nero. In the 15th century it was largely rebuilt and for the following two centuries the plan of the Basilica was constantly revised. The St Peter's we see today owes most of its design to the inspiration of Michelangelo (who died before the work was completed). However, the Basilica's present plan – a Latin cross surmounted by a dome (designed and largely built by Michelangelo), with a splendid façade (by Maderna) and two semi-circular colon-nades (by Bernini) lining an enormous piazza – took more than 150 years to complete and demanded the talents of such architects and artists as Bramante, Raphael, de Sangallo, Maderno and Bernini. The dimensions of the Basilica are immense; the façade alone is 115 metres long and 45 metres high and the interior can hold up to 60,000 people and contains a multitude of treasures, both artistic and religious. Among them are Michelangelo's Pietà, Bernini's baldacchino over the high altar, Canova's monument to Pope Clement XIII and St. Peter's throne by Bernini. St. Peter's Basilica is the heart of the Roman Catholic Church and attracts millions of visitors and pilgrims every year (the 13th century bronze statue of St. Peter is the focus of pilgrims' veneration and his right foot has been almost entirely worn away by their kisses). Charlemagne and other later Holy Roman Emperors were crowned here and the Pope celebrates mass here (only he can celebrate at the high altar), both inside the Basilica and outside in the piazza.

Until the late 20th century, the visitor to St Peter's would emerge abruptly into the vast expanse of the piazza from a maze of tiny medieval streets, but in the 1920s Mussolini built a grand avenue (V. di Concilliazione) from the piazza down to the river Tiber.

Museo del Vatican (Vatican Museum)

(Entrance from the Piazza S. Pietro. Tel: (0)6698 3333)

The Vatican Museums house one of the worlds' most important collections of art. The galleries house collections of ancient, Renaissance and modern sculpture, painting and decorative arts as well as artefacts and historical Papal objects. It also leads the way to La Capella Sistina (the Sistine Chapel). Pope Sixtus IV created the chapel and in 1508 he commissioned Michelangelo to decorate the ceiling with scenes from the Old Testament. Michelangelo added a fresco of the Last Judgement above the altar in 1534. The frescoes on the walls, which were completed before the ceiling, were painted between 1481 and 1483 by a team of painters including Botticelli, Ghirlandaio, Pinturicchio and Signorelli. The College of Cardinals uses the chapel as a chamber when they go into secret session to elect a new Pope.

FURTHER READING

Bull, G., *Inside the Vatican*. London, 1982

Cardinale, I., *The Holy See and the International Order*. Gerrards Cross, 1976

Mayer, F. *et al, The Vatican: Portrait of a State and a Community*. Dublin, 1980

Nichols, P., *The Pope's Divisions*. London, 1981

Reese. T., *Inside the Vatican*. Harvard University Press, 1997

Walsh, M. J., *Vatican City State*. [Bibliography] Oxford and Santa Barbara
    (CA), 1983

Vatican Website: www.vatican.va